ABOVE US ONLY SKY

The Religion of Ordinary Life

DON CUPITT

POLEBRIDGE PRESS
Santa Rosa, California

Cover and interior design by Robaire Ream

Library of Congress Cataloging-in-Publication Data
Cupitt, Don.
 Above us only sky : the religion of ordinary life / Don Cupitt.
    p. cm.
 Includes bibliographical references and index.
 ISBN 978-1-59815-011-7
 1. Religion--Philosophy. 2. Religion--Forecasting. I. Title.
 BL51.C815 2008
 210--dc22
                                                      2008032434

Contents

SOLAR LIVING AND CULTURAL RENEWAL

PRESENTISM

Preface

In the age of globalization people, money, ideas and goods are moving around from country to country on an enormous scale. It is expedient that 'the system', the way everything works, shall be more or less the same everywhere; and so it is now, to an astonishing degree. The calendar, social administration, the cash economy, science and technology, the education and health systems, transport and the media are very similar in most places. Increasingly, there is a single global culture and a single worldwide conversation of humanity.

In addition to all this, the United Nations Organization and the Universal Declaration of Human Rights, together with various liberal democratic, humanitarian and socialist traditions, have gone some way towards giving us a single world moral vocabulary.

But do we have a single world *religion*? The ancient faith-traditions that are conventionally described as 'world religions' are all of them of local origin, tied to particular languages and peoples, and in many ways long past their best. Around the world they are nowadays chiefly conspicuous when being used to add sectarian venom to local conflicts. The reputation of organized religion has plummeted, and it is not surprising that so many liberals now feel that they have been too tolerant of it for too long. Religion is a serious threat to human well-being, and from now on people of good will should do all they can to diminish its influence upon public life at every level, local, national and international.

I now accept almost all the criticisms of organized religion that are coming from people like Sam Harris (*The End of Faith*, 2004). But I dispute the claim that there isn't and there cannot be any truly global religion, because I believe that a new and truly global religious consciousness has in recent decades been quietly easing itself in around the world. It does not need any visible organization and does not make any special non-rational doctrinal claims. It is the religion of ordinary life, a secular, purely this-worldly, and radically-democratic affirmation just of ordinary life, on the part of people who no longer feel any need to 'look up' to any sort of higher authority, whether traditional, or cosmic, or social. Its cultural background is Christian: it is secular-Protestant, and post-ideological: its main intellectual task is to explain how it can affirm life so ardently in an age as troubled and even nihilistic as our time is.

I first discovered this new religion in 1998/99 (*The New Religion of Life in Everyday Speech*, 1999), and tried to demonstrate its arrival in our ordinary-language idioms. For about the past dozen years I have, in a string of books,[1] been trying to get clearer about what it is, what it involves and whether it is indeed the long-awaited truly-global religious outlook. In this present book a systematic account of it is attempted. Remember that I am not trying to foist *my* objectionable ideas upon *you:* no, I am trying to show you what you already think, or are coming to think. This new religion is neither revealed to us by a god, nor invented by any individual founder: it is what is currently emerging in the world-wide conversation of all humanity. *We ourselves* are currently creating the one true faith, at last. It is simply a passionate religious feeling just for life itself, the fray.

The new religion is solar living: we accept and we joyfully affirm life and its limits, traditionally described as Time, Chance, and Death. We no longer wish to veil the truth about life, nor do we dream of somehow being able to transcend its limits. Instead, our religion is now our joyful and immediate engagement with life, just as it is.

This means that we have given up belief in a supernatural world in which we used to locate our first origin, the source of present help, and our last home. In the process, we have been reluctantly compelled to break with the received ecclesiastical form of Christianity, which places great emphasis upon supernatural belief and upon the church's structures of authority. Traditional Christianity is now our Old Testament, valuable to us even though outdated, because study of it and of its history shows us where we have come from, and how we have become what we now are.

Nevertheless, in an important sense we remain Christians. After the end of supernatural belief and of the church's authority, the Christian tradition still lives and is still developing rapidly. Since the end of World War II the Christian spirit of critical thinking, of systematic *self*-criticism and perpetual reform, has spread around the whole world in modern science, technology, critical history, and liberal democracy, just as the Christian ethic has spread similarly in our discourse about human rights and our humanitarian feeling. This Christian ethic was from the beginning based upon the idea that the government of human life by Divine Law is now superseded by something far better, and now at last we see the full implications of that idea. Christianity is, and has been since Jesus and Paul, a tradition in which theistic religion turns into religious humanism, and God becomes man. In the process an ethic of human-fellow-feeling replaces the old ethic of Divine Law.

Thus, in completing its historical task, ecclesiastical Christianity comes to an end, and we find ourselves to be post-Christians who are still Christians—albeit in a new, this worldly and quite non-sectarian way.

Don Cupitt Cambridge, 2007

The Religion of Ordinary Life

Almost all of religion hitherto has been based on a clear distinction between two great realms, the profane world of everyday, secular human life and the sacred world. Various bits of the everyday world were designated 'holy' because they mediated contact or interaction between the two worlds. Thus there were a holy land, a holy people, a sacred language, sacred writings, holy places, buildings, rituals and so on. It was somehow desperately important to secure the favour and the blessing of the spirits and gods, and the various appointed channels through which you could access divine presence, forgiveness, and grace were very highly regarded.

The question arises, why was secular life somehow unendurable or impossible without supernatural favour? Why was the mighty apparatus of religious mediation so important? Briefly, it appears that human beings were very anxious and very needy. Our ignorance, our sense of the precariousness of life, and the certainty of death were so overwhelming that almost no human being could contemplate, head-on and calmly, the facts of the human condition, and then go on to live a contented, autonomous secular life. Human beings simply could not bear to live without very elaborate protective fictions and the whole apparatus of mediated religion.

In modern times—and especially since about 1850—everything has changed. The sacred world of religion and the everyday human life-world have merged and have become identical. It feels like the end of history, in rather the same way and for much the same reasons as the gradual decay of monarchy and caste or class society, and the emergence of liberal democracy as the last form of political organisation, also feels (to some, at least) like the end of history. Indeed, you may say that in both cases what's happened is that certain great disciplinary institutions that used to be thought of as 'absolutes', and as permanently necessary to human well-being, have now come to the end of their useful life. We don't need them any more: we can manage on our own.

In the case of religion, I am suggesting that the end of religion as we have so far known it comes when people no longer need to be governed by religious law, nor to be supported by stories and beliefs about supernatural beings.[2] Religion instead becomes immediate: it's now about your attitude to your own life, and the way you see it as fitting into the larger stream of human life in general.[3] It is about the way you negotiate your own deal with life and its basic conditions: its temporality, its precariousness, your freedom, and your coming death. It is about how we can find eternal joy just in the mere living of our ordinary lives. We no longer 'look up' in any way at all: we've learnt the trick of living so intensely that we do not expect ever again to be seriously troubled by the old fears.

This event is forecast in the Bible, for example in the prophet Jeremiah's promise of a new covenant and in the account of the Day of Pentecost in the *Acts of the Apostles*, and also by the long tradition of talk about the coming of the Kingdom of God on earth. In the later Christian tradition the secular realm begins to assert itself in the late Middle Ages, in seventeenth-century Protestantism in countries like Holland, and above all in the emergence of liberal democracy and the middle-class leadership of industrial society after the French Revolution. After about 1870, with rising prosperity and better sanitation, ordinary urban life is suddenly innocent, and different. But perhaps the most striking recent manifestation of 'the new religion of life' was the height of protest-and-pop youth culture in the late 1960s. Tradition and the authority of the older generation died, and Europe became a whole lot more secular than before. Organized religion has been in galloping decline ever since.

Elsewhere I have argued that one of the best ways to convince sceptics of the reality of the changes I am describing is to study the flood of new idioms about life that have entered the language in the last forty years. It seems undeniable that a great deal of religious attention has now been transferred from God to life. Life itself—as we see in the later writings of the critic F. R. Leavis—has become the religious object. I need to come to terms with life, I need to gain control over my own life, I need to live my own life in my own way, I need to enjoy what people call 'the feeling of being alive', and I need to love life intensely, and live it to its fullest. A kind of heroic, courageous faith in life and a determination to engage with it and make the most of it is the gateway to victory over anxiety and death, and will show us how we can find 'life-satisfaction' in making our own modest contribution to the building (and also the renewal) of the common human life-world.

That's the agenda, in brief. I don't need to write any apologetics for this new universal human religion, because it is now quietly slipping into place all over the world. It needs no help from me, nor from anyone else. But I do want to present its 'systematic theology' as shortly and as clearly as I possibly can, so that people can see a little better what we are losing, and what we are gaining. Here then is a very brief outline, with a few marginal comments. As you read it, remember that my claim is that most or all of this you already know. I'm not pretending to be introducing anything at all odd or unheard-of. What I am presenting is already mostly platitudinous.

1

LIFE

1. **Life is everything.**

    Life is the whole human world, everything as it looks to and is experienced by the only beings who actually have a world, namely human beings with a life to live.

2. **Life is all there is.**

    Our age is now post-metaphysical. The world of life is not dependent upon, nor derived from, any other realm, nor is there any other world after it, or beyond it.

3. **Life has no outside.**

    Everything is immanent, interconnected, secondary. Everything remains within life. When we are born, we don't come *into* this world, and when we die we don't *leave* it. There is no absolute point of view from which someone can see 'the Truth', the final Truth, about life.

4. **Life is God.**

    Life is that in which 'we live and move and have our being' (Acts 17:28), within which we are formed, and of whose past we will remain part. Both our ultimate Origin and our Last End are within life. Life is now as God to us.

5. **To love life is to love God.**

    Every bit of our life is final for us, and we should treat all life as a sacred gift and responsibility. We should see our relation to life as being like an immediate relation to God. We are moved and touched by the way all living things, and not just we ourselves, spontaneously love life, affirm it and cling to it.

6. **Life is a continuous streaming process of symbolic expression and exchange.**

    The motion of language logically precedes the appearing of a formed and 'definite' world. It is in this sense that it was once said that 'In the beginning was the Word'.

2

LIFE AND MY LIFE

7. **My life is my own personal stake in life.**

   The traditional relation of the soul to God is now experienced in
   the form of the relation between my life and life in general. As,
   traditionally, one's first responsibility in religion was for the salvation of one's own soul, so now a human being's first duty is the
   duty to recognise that I simply am the life I have lived so far, plus
   the life that still remains to me.

8. **My life is all I have, and all I'll ever have.**

   I must *own* my own life, in three senses: I must claim it wholly as
   mine, acknowledge it, and assume full responsibility for the way
   I conduct it. I must live my own life in a way that is authentically
   mine. To be authentically oneself in this way—the opposite of
   'living a lie'—is the first part of the contribution each of us should
   seek to make to life as a whole.

9. **Every human person has, in principle, an equal stake in life.**

   This principle is vital to our ideas of justice and of love for the
   fellow-human being. Murder and other offences against the person
   are almost everywhere regarded as equally serious, whoever the
   victim is. The love of God is love and fellow-feeling for 'the neigh-
   bour'—or the fellow creature—generalized without limit until it
   becomes the love of all life.

10. **In human relationships, justice is first in order, but love is first in
    value.**

   We should esteem love most highly of all; but love itself must be
   based on justice, not least in parental/filial and in sexual relationships. The work of justice is to clear a level space for love.

3

THE LIMITS OF LIFE

11. **Life is subject to limits. In life, everything is subject to temporality.**
    In life everything is held within and is subject to the movement of
    one-way linear time. Life is, as people say, a single ticket: there are
    no second chances or retakes.

12. **In life, everything is contingent.**
    In life, the one-way linear movement of time makes every moment
    final and every chance a last chance; but at the same time every-
    thing is contingent. This painful combination of finality with
    contingency is what gives rise to people's talk of luck or fate. More
    to the point, it also follows that there are no fixed or unchanging
    absolutes in life. There are no clearly and permanently fixed reali-
    ties, or identities, or even standards.

13. **Life itself, and everything in the world of life, is mediated by
    language.**
    Consciousness is an effect of the way language lights up the world
    of experience, and self-consciousness is an effect of the use of
    language to talk about itself. Thought is an incompletely-executed
    motion of language somewhere in our heads.

14. **Life goes on, but my life is finite.**
    The only deaths we need to prepare ourselves for are the deaths
    of others who are dear to us. We will never experience our own
    deaths. So we should simply love life and say Yes to life until our
    last day. There is no point at all in making any other preparation
    for death.

4

FAITH IN LIFE

15. **When I have faith in life, love life, and commit myself to it, I have bought a package deal: life with its limits.**

    Whereas in traditional theology 'evil' was seen as a secondary intruder into an originally perfect world, and therefore as being eliminable, the limits of life, which were traditionally called 'metaphysical evil' or 'evils of imperfection', are essential to life. Unlike God, life is finite and imperfect, and has to be accepted as being neither more nor less than what it is. If I want to refuse the package, the alternative for me is 'passive nihilism' or thoroughgoing pessimism. For the religion of life, apologetics takes the form of an attempt to show that pessimism is unreasonable.

16. **The package deal of life cannot be renegotiated.**

    There is nobody to renegotiate the deal with. We cannot hope to vary the terms on which life is offered to us.

17. **Life is bittersweet, and bittersweetness is greatly to be preferred to pure sweetness.**

    In the classic iconography of Heaven, everyone is 33 years old, everyone looks the same, and everything is oddly dead, like a plastic flower on a grave. In real life, we love imperfections, irregularities, beauty spots, and signs of frailty or age. The mortal actual is far more loveable than the ideal.

18. **We should never complain, nor even feel any need to complain.**

    Life should be loved purely affirmatively and exactly as it is. Everyone gets basically the same deal, and nothing else is on offer. Any sense of victimhood or paranoia or grievance is out of place, and we should get it out of our systems. Never say, nor even *think* 'Why me?'

5

SOLAR LIVING

19. Life is a gift (with no giver) that is renewed every day, and true religion is expressive, 'solar' living.

By faith, and without any qualification or restriction, I should let life well up in me and pour itself out into symbolic expression through me. Thus I 'get myself together': we become ourselves by expressing ourselves.

20. Solarity is creative living-by-dying.

In solar living I live by dying because I am passing away all the time. In my symbolic expression I get myself together, but as I do so I must instantly pass on and leave that self behind. I must not be *attached* to my own life, nor to my own products, or expressed selves. My self, and all my loves, must be continuously let go of and continuously renewed. Dying therefore no longer has any terrors for me, because I have made a way of life out of it.

21. Solar living creates great joy and happiness.

My symbolic expression may take various forms, as it pours out in my quest for selfhood, in my loves or my work. In all these areas, continuous letting-go and renewal creates joy, which on occasion rises and spills over into cosmic happiness. This 'cosmic' happiness is the modern equivalent of the traditional Summum Bonum, the 'chief end' of life.

22. Even the Supreme Good must be left behind at once.

I, all my expressions, and even the Summun Bonum, the Supreme Good itself, are all of them transient. Eternal happiness may be great enough to make one feel that one's whole life has been worthwhile, but it is utterly transient. Let it go!

6

THE END OF
'THE REAL WORLD'

What people call 'reality' is merely an effect of either power, or habit.

23. **The Real: a product of lazy, unthinking habits of perception and interpretation.**

    The fixity and unchangeability that people like to ascribe to the real world out there is in fact merely the effect upon them of their own lazy habits. They are in a rut of their own making.

24. **There is no readymade Reality out there.**

    There is no readymade meaningfulness out there, and no objective Truth out there. Meaning is found only in language, and truth belongs only to true statements. Because life is always language-wrapped, everything in the world of life is always shaped by the language in which we describe it, and in a living language everything is always changing. It follows that we ourselves, and our language, and our world, are shifting all the time like the sea. Nothing is, nor can it be, objectively and permanently fixed.

25. **We ourselves are the only Creator.**

    As we become critically aware, the objective world melts away. So many supposed features of the world turn out to be merely features of the language in which we describe it. By now, critical thinking has dissolved away objective reality, leaving us with just the human world-wide web, the stream of all our human activity and conversation, and the changing consensus-world-picture that it generates. Our world is our communal, partly-botched work of folk art.

26. **Nihilism and creative freedom.**

    There is no stable real world and no enduring real self. But this situation is not one for despair: it offers us the freedom to remake ourselves and our world. By solar living we can each of us make a personal offering, a small contribution to life, an oblation.

7

DEATH

27. Passing out into life.
> Unattached, but loving life to the last, I am able at the end of my life to pass out into the moving flow of life in general. The only sensible preparation for death is the practice of solar living.

* * * * *

In 27 brief slogans, I have tried to present a short systematic theology of the religion of life that (I think) most people in the West already believe, or are coming to believe. It is already built into our everyday speech. Some people may prefer to describe it as a philosophy of life (German, *Lebensphilosophie*). Other people may wish to think of it as the final stage of the historical development of religion, to which Christianity itself looks forward, under such slogans as the nineteenth-century phrase 'building the Kingdom of God on earth'. I don't mind: I don't think it matters too much, and I certainly would not wish to privilege either any particular doctrinal formulation or any particular technical terms.

Backing
and
Backup

Philosophy

1

CRITICAL THINKING

Most of the long-established 'world religions' developed in close association with traditions of philosophy, and to this day you still need a little philosophy in order to understand their central ideas correctly. For example, you need to understand the metaphysical attributes of God—his infinity, eternity, simplicity, impassibility and so on—in order to be clear that the God of Jews, Christians and Muslims is utterly different from the old Sky Father of Bronze-Age religion, who was variously called Zeus or Jupiter, Wotan or Odin, and so on. In turn, if you do not recognize the infinite difference between God and Zeus, then you may also fail to see the equally great difference between the sense in which, in Christianity, Jesus Christ is the 'Son' of God, and the sense in which the demigod Heracles/Hercules is the son of Zeus/Jupiter.

The consequences of such a failure can be painful. A Christian known to me was recently shocked to be told by a British Muslim: 'You Christians believe that God had sex with the Virgin Mary, and that Jesus was his son'. The remark illustrates not only the fact that many Muslims, having no philosophy at all nowadays and even less knowledge of Christianity, see Christianity as a pagan religion, but also that modern Christians have themselves become so bereft of philosophy, and so crude in their language about God and Christ, that their religion often deserves and invites the Muslim's caricature.

In short, the standard ethical monotheism common to Jews, Christians and Muslims never came to us simply by God's own self-revelation. It already presupposed philosophy. It developed slowly over several centuries, beginning just after the time of Alexander the Great, and reaching completion after the Council of Nicea in the fourth century C.E., first in the Greek theologians, and then most influentially in St Augustine of Hippo. This orthodox doctrine of God involved a marriage of Moses and Plato, as Jewish writing about God was worked up into a system by a line of philosophically-minded writers in the tradition of Plato such as Philo, Clement, Proclus and Plotinus. At the height of the Middle Ages Jewish, Christian and Arabic philosophers all shared the same Greek metaphysical idea of God. It was so influential for so long that to this day some people still speak of late or 'Neo'-Platonism as 'the perennial philosophy' that (they think) underlies all or most of the great world religions.

To understand 'traditional' religious belief, then, you have to learn something about the later platonic philosophy; but now arises a complication, because Plato is *also* our chief early source for another great tradition in Western thought, namely the tradition of critical thinking founded chiefly by Socrates. It is ironical that Plato gave us *both* the metaphysics that nourished and fattened up Christianity *and* the dialectical or questioning style of thinking that was eventually to break Christianity down.

Critical thinking is the glory of the West. It questions everything, including itself. Nothing can expect to go on being taken for granted: everything must have its credentials ready for inspection. This habit of testing all claims to knowledge and all assumptions was developed by a line of critical philosophers of whom the greatest are (arguably) Socrates, Descartes, Kant, Nietzsche and Derrida. It gave us freedom of thought and expression. It gave us by-products that include orthodox scientific method and the critical historical method. It gave us our wealthy science-based industrial civilization, and our liberal democratic kind of society. It is what our modern universities have been all about for the past one-and-a-half centuries (in the English-speaking world), or two-and-a-half-centuries (in the German-speaking world). Because it regards *everything* as questionable, it has gradually exposed and fatally undermined layer after layer of the myths and deep assumptions that have hitherto shaped the ways we have seen the world. We have thus lost all the old 'absolutes' and 'certainties', as people call them, and have become very emptied-out and free. The former 'real world' has come to be replaced by our current world-*picture*, now seen as being very lightweight and provisional. A prominent friend and colleague of mine, John Milbank, who remains devoted to the old dogmatic kind of religious faith, declares that philosophy leads to nihilism, which in his view is a very bad thing. He therefore rejects philosophy and turns instead to the reaffirmation of orthodox religious dogma. An upmarket, neo-con version of fundamentalism, you might say.

I take the opposite view. Critical thinking really is the glory of the West, and we must go all the way with it. It dissolves away reality, including the reality of one's own self, and leads to an emptied-out, spiritually-liberated condition that I call 'Empty radical humanism' (using the word Empty in the Buddhist sense, to deny that the self is a substance). My life is my own work of art, and the world around us is our communal, ever-changing world of folk art, graffiti-encrusted as the New York subway. We are our own self-expression, and we make it all up. There's nothing but the fountain-flow of possibility into Be-ing, and of ourselves into expression. Here is the basis for a new beginning in religion that may unite East and West: a this-worldly, expressivist, post-Christian post-Buddhism.

More of that as we go along. For the present, we return to the question of the sources of the Western critical kind of thinking, for it needs to be pointed out that we did not learn it solely from the great philosophers. Two other sources are very important. The first is the *law court*, which in classical antiquity was one of the great nurseries of reason. How can we purport to establish publicly just what happened in the past? What is evidence, and how do we assess its credibility? How are arguments marshalled in support of one particular reconstruction of past events? How can we judge a particular piece of behaviour to have been *intentional?* All this is complicated enough, but suppose that you are an advocate presenting your case: not only must you make your own presentation as persuasive as you can, but also as you speak you need to remember that your opponent, the advocate for the other side, is listening intently to everything you say in the hope of detecting loopholes, weak points in your argument that he can exploit. You are forced to become self-critical, because you know that the world of the law court is a theatre of conflicting interpretations, and that all the materials that you are so confidently arranging into one pattern may be arranged into a very different pattern by your ingenious rival when he gets his turn to speak.

The law court was thus one arena in which the critical kind of thinking could be developed. Another, also much emphasized by Nietzsche, was the religious believer's scrupulous *self-examination before God*, 'unto whom all hearts be open, all desires known, and from whom no secrets are hid'. God scans us infallibly, and to become fit for his presence we must strenuously seek both intellectual and moral integrity, rooting out all the convenient forgetting, the self-deception, and the wishful thinking that normally enable us to live with ourselves. Nietzsche thought that this imperative was a major factor in Christianity's eventual downfall, as 'Christian dogma was destroyed by Christian ethics'. Christian scrupulosity eventually forces people to admit that they can no longer believe Christian dogma. Yes, indeed: but the theme has a wider application, for we see just the same scrupulosity very clearly in Charles Darwin, as he anxiously collects, takes account of, and thanks people for all the facts and arguments, pro and con, that they send him. Like a very good journalist, Darwin desperately wanted to get it as right as it could be got, and was ready to take endless pains, so that when it finally appeared *The Origin of Species* was exceptionally well-prepared. He was as grateful for a difficulty as he was for a bit of confirmation—and that is the true critical spirit.

Critical thinking is, I say again, the glory of the West. But most of us do not love it: we hate the idea of going all the way with it because we fear the nihilism to which it seems to lead.

Recently, Orhan Pamuk and others have said that in the Middle East people want to cherry-pick Western culture. They want Western medicine, they want modern Western weaponry, and they want all the new information and entertainment technologies—but without *themselves* having to go through the profound spiritual and cultural changes that alone made it possible to develop all these things. But people should be ashamed to wear a quartz watch without being able to explain exactly how it works. And so on—but now it occurs to us that nowadays *we westerners also want to cherry-pick 'the West'*. We don't really like critical thinking, and we pay it only the most perfunctory respect, because we dread its long-term effect upon all our most-cherished moral, philosophical and religious illusions. This is true even in the case of medicine, where one might have thought that the huge benefits already gained by sticking rigorously to scientific method were most undeniable; but most of us are like Prince Charles, who after rather briefly and grudgingly acknowledging the existence of 'ortho-dox', 'traditional' medicine moves swiftly on to sing the praises of 'comple-mentary', wish-fulfilment medicine which may not actually *work*, but does make you feel good. He can swallow the bitter pill of reason only if it is coated with a thick sugary coat of the unreason that he loves best.

Most of us are like that, warily accepting the need for critical thinking and scientific method in certain areas of life and for part of the time, but otherwise gratefully relapsing into a warmer and more practicable world-view. Especially where matters of religion, spirituality and morality are con-cerned. We love to deceive ourselves.

Religion is the crux. All five of the great philosophers named earlier had rather uneasy relations with religion. Socrates was condemned to death for supposedly corrupting the young by his teaching. Descartes, like Spinoza, chose to live quietly in what was at that time Europe's most tolerant country, and was careful not to include religion within the scope of his method of universal doubt. Even Kant, despite his fame during his own lifetime, felt that he had to be cautious. European intellectuals were long scarred by the memory of the way Galileo had been treated.

By Nietzsche's day critical thinking, together with the right to almost unlimited freedom of thought and expression, was well established, and he himself went further into philosophical nihilism ('we must remake everything as art') than any of his predecessors. Then, amazingly, Derrida found ways of going further yet. But both in Nietzsche and in Derrida there is what the financial markets call 'a dead cat bounce'. They drop into nihilism so suddenly and startlingly that in both of them there is a rebound, an indirect and negative return of religious ideas *after nihilism*. When we have tracked down and evicted every one of the deep metaphysical assumptions that used to make belief in the actual existence of God seem true; when our world-picture has at last become fully and permanently non-theistic, *then* God can become conspicuous again by his very absence. A completely God-forsaken place still reminds us, negatively, of the non-existent God. So, in spite of their scepticism, Nietzsche still ends with a sort-of theology of redemption, and Derrida with a theology of the divine impossibility.[4] Even today, the great philosophers leave us with some possibility of religious thought. (The names of Wittgenstein and Heidegger may be added here in support.) But it will of course be a religious thought very different from the religious thought of medieval, or even early-modern, times.

All this is topical in relation to the violent lurch towards highly militant neo-conservative or 'fundamentalist' religion in so many parts of the world today. This has happened because, until about 1968, liberal-minded religious people commonly claimed that a 'critical orthodoxy' was possible. You could in good conscience embrace critical thinking, and in particular the study of theology by the historical-critical method, and yet remain orthodox in your personal faith. Organized religion wouldn't have to change very much. So until the 1960s liberal professors and bishops complacently considered themselves to be *both* sound and solid churchmen *and* intellectually up-to-date. They looked down upon the Evangelicals, who in those days smarted with a painful, and entirely justified, sense of their own inferiority.

Then at the end of the Sixties the liberal 'synthesis' collapsed. It became clear that all those professedly liberal theologians and bishops paid only lip-service to critical thinking. They didn't practise it at all, for when under pressure they all became authoritarian. Worse, they did not actually have any worked-out and coherent fundamental theology of their own to set before the public. The Evangelicals, who openly and honestly rejected critical thinking, at least had a faith to defend which (despite its being totally irrational) could claim to be approximately coherent and 'traditional'. So liberalism died, and the only orthodox Christians left are pre-critical Evangelicals or Catholics. In other religions it has been decided that the traditional belief-system can be read as coherent and practicable by a modern person only if it is read as a political ideology and a charter for freedom-fighters. Zionism could thus be seen as a coherent, up-to-date and effective modern reading of Judaism. 'Moderate' religious Judaism still exists, but it is relatively so weak as to be negligible, and it is currently disappearing by assimilation. Similarly, militant revolutionary Islamism is now the only coherent, up-to-date and effectual modern reading of Islamic faith. The moderate, apolitical version of Islam that is so hopefully invoked by our politicians is intellectually and socially negligible. It is on the way out. Only extremism actually works; and the same story can be told about Sikhism, Hinduism and the rest. Moderate, liberal religion is dead because it never really had the guts to be consistently critical or self-critical. It was always hopelessly timorous and self-interested.

In this book we accept that critical thinking is indeed the glory of the West. 'The only game in town' is to go all the way with it. It will wipe out traditional organized religion, of course. Old-style 'religions' are dead. But there is something new *after* nihilism, and (as we'll see in detail) it is already emerging in the language of ordinary people.

2

KNOWLEDGE

Much more than any other of our senses, the sense of sight seems to present us with a finished, complete and highly-wrought world. Look around you: the visual field seems to be a plenum, with no apparent gaps in it. As you turn around full circle and look up and down, you never come to the edge of the visual field. Almost everything you see falls into one or another of a wide range of natural kinds, animal, vegetable, mineral, meteorological and so on. (Meteorology is literally 'the science of things on high', and at one time might include the heavenly bodies, as well as clouds and so forth.) Consider also the various regular cycles of the days, the month, the seasons and so on, and we see how natural it was in prescientific times for human beings to conclude that they had been placed within a *cosmos*, a readymade, rationally-ordered and unified world.

At every point within it the world seems to be equally complex and finely-wrought: nowhere is the detail skimped. But what a person has made with his own hand, he knows 'like the back of his hand'. So it was common in prescientific times to see the world, not only as having been made and as at every point manifesting its Maker's handiwork, but also as being everywhere pervaded by the divine reason or Logos, by the divine Wisdom, or the divine Spirit. The world rested upon God's power, which kept it in being; and the world also rested within God's complete knowledge of it. But the human mind has been created as a finite image and counterpart of the divine Mind, so that the way *we* think and know the world parallels on a small scale, and participates in, God's absolute knowledge of the world that he has made. We could therefore be sure of the objectivity of our knowledge of the world because it is, as one might say, always 'embedded within' God's eternal and absolute knowledge.

Such is, or was, 'realism'—the traditional popular conviction of the objectivity of our knowledge of a readymade real world, out there and inde-pendent of us. Realism depended upon the doctrine of the creation of the world by God. Theology got us across the gap between what we seem to perceive through our senses, and what is or may be out there objectively.

With the birth of a new mathematical physics in the thought of Gal-ileo and Descartes everything began to change. All talk of 'final causes' or immanent purposiveness was abruptly banished from science, and the physical universe was henceforth to be described in terms of matter, motion, and number only. The universe was to be seen as an elegant clock-work machine. So Descartes constructed the new physics as a working mathematical model of the world; but how was he to establish the actual existence of a mind-independent world out there, of which the manmade model is a true copy?

To maintain the traditional realism at this point, Descartes appeals to God. He implicitly admits that our sense-experiences and our formulation of the laws of nature don't by themselves give us sufficient reason to be quite certain of the world's actual existence outside our minds; but, he says, I know that God has created my mind: I know that he has implanted in me a firm conviction of the objective reality of the world; and I know that God has the power to create the world; so I conclude that God must indeed have created a real world out there, of which the new physics gives a true account.

Thus Descartes borrowed from the old theology to keep the old realism going for almost another century, with some interesting consequences: physicists even to this day still usually see their own subject as demanding realism. In order to maintain the seriousness and the intellectual beauty of modern physics and, still more, in order to keep up its social authority and its funding from the public purse, it *must* take a realist view of its own theories and the claims they make. The effect of this is that physics commonly remains crypto-theistic to this day. Like the Church in former times, it has to be realist for political reasons, and all forms of realism in the long run need to be founded in realistic theism. God is the long stop, the ultimate Guarantor of every profession's claim to possess objective knowledge.

Descartes' timorousness and theological conservatism thus helped to shape power relations between theology and physics that still trouble us today. But of course philosophy did not stop with Descartes. In the next century, the eighteenth, Hume and Kant began to ask the great question: Can we justify realism, and the objectivity of human knowledge of the world, purely immanently—i.e., just from within our own human perspective, and *without* invoking God's absolute knowledge to underpin it? Hume answered: No, but we do still have our inextinguishable natural *belief* in objectivity. Kant answered: Within limits, Yes. In order to have a world at all, and in order to gain the scientific knowledge we do undoubtedly have, we have no choice but to construct our world in the way we do.

We can't actually step out of our own heads in order to check the objectivity of our own knowledge, but from *inside* our heads we have no choice but to work upon a realist presumption. Kant's arguments depend upon his belief in the finality of Aristotle's logic, Euclid's geometry, and Newton's ideas of space, time, matter and motion. If these things were all permanently compulsory Kant might possibly be right, but towards the end of the nineteenth century they all went into the melting-pot. Nevertheless, a moderate, historicized or 'sociological' version of Kant's doctrine can still be put forward. It says that we have little choice but to go along with, and accept sort-of-realistically, the assumptions about the existence of the common world and the objectivity of our knowledge that are built into the common language of our own time.

My story is a little different again. *As an individual*, I'm an aestheticist, and a believer in *homo artifex*, the human artist. There is no purely-objective reality or truth. We make it all up: we can't get out of our dream altogether, but we can try to dream up more useful and better dreams. However, someone who is trying to articulate a common faith for a group needs something cooler than that. We'll say, *we* never have THE world absolutely, for we are always inside OUR world—that is, our own human perspective. We can never make a direct comparison between OUR world and THE world, because we can't get out of our own heads in order to find a standpoint from which we can see both OUR world and THE world, and compare the two. We have in effect only OUR world: but there's nothing wrong with that. OUR construction of the world works, for now: that's why we have it. There is every reason to stick to scientific method and the scientific world-picture, because it does after all work, and works very well. So we will not go far wrong if, for most of the time, we are content simply to accept OUR world, and go along with it. But we need to be ready to accept change, and sometimes even to instigate change. We have no good reason to think that our present world-picture will turn out to be permanently true; in fact, precedent suggests that science keeps changing and will go on changing.

This implies that in our conception of knowledge we have come a long way since the good old days when we could live forever in The Truth because our human knowledge participated in and was embedded in God's absolute knowledge of this world. Today we have only 'weak', pragmatic, temporary knowledge: we go along with the current consensus. It's true for now because it works for now. So we'll work with it, just for now, until the moment comes when we think it is time to have a go at changing it.

The hinge between the two conceptions of knowledge is not only Kant; it is also Darwin. The older kind of human being had the mind of an angel, a mind like God's, and heavenly contemplation was the highest kind of knowledge. Today we live after Darwin, and we have the mind of a clever animal. In thinking of knowledge we nowadays think first about the things an animal must learn if it is to survive. A collection of skills that have proved useful in helping us to find our way around, accomplish our purposes, and survive: that's knowledge, now.

All this means that in philosophy and religion we need to give up the old platonic idea that the Summum Bonum, the highest good, the chief end of human life, is a kind of *knowledge*, and, in particular, a divine and blessedness-giving kind of knowledge, the pure intellectual contemplation of God. *Gloria Dei vivens homo: vita hominis Visio Dei* (the glory of God is a living man, and the life of man is the Vision of God). This ancient conception of the Summum Bonum makes knowledge the highest value, and the intuition of eternal necessity of being the most profoundly satisfying kind of knowledge. But it was all tied up with what now seems a preposterously intellectualist and supernaturalist picture of what a human being is. In those days we were almost angels, and there was a pre-established harmony between the world-order and the way we think. But today we have come down in the world drastically. Me, I'm just a talking animal, and so are you. What makes me happy is just love, and occasional joy in creative work. My biggest long-term need is for the religious faith to love life and say Yes to life with all my heart. I need to be able to look without fear at the basic limits of life, and to accept the whole thing as a package deal, so that prospective physical decline and death do not get me down. Thus I've traded in the old visionary 'eternalist' conception of knowledge for a much more modest view of what knowledge is, and for the view that our salvation lies in solar living, solar loving. It's a pretty good bargain. It's not The Truth, because there is no Truth, but it's true enough for me and for you.

3

TRUTH

Two distinct ideas about truth are prominent in ordinary language.

The first may be called factual. Truth is the quality or state of being true: that is, being in accordance with fact or reality. The objects that may be described as true in this sense may include acts of witness, as well as particular factual assertions, generalizations, beliefs, hypotheses, theories and even whole bodies of knowledge and subject-areas. To be accepted as true a disputed item needs to be able to survive the test-procedure generally accepted as being appropriate in that area. Such test-procedures include in particular standard scientific method, the critical historical method, and full-scale trial in a court of law. Applying the test involves at least checking out all the publicly-available evidence pro and con, whether it be experimental evidence, or the testimony of a witness, or historical documents. A disputed item that has come through such testing successfully may fairly be accounted part of society's stock of public knowledge, and is therefore eligible to be taught in schools and colleges, and to be acted upon by public bodies with decisions to make. Truth here is the current consensus about what works, or (as an excellent idiom has it), what we should **go on**.

Modern developed societies have, and act upon, an enormously-large body of publicly-established truth of this sort. But it does not play a very prominent part in religion or morality, or in the actual living of most people's everyday lives, where the word 'truth' is nearly always used to imply loyalty, reliability and trustworthiness—in short, *moral* truth. In this connexion we use idioms like **ringing true** (authentic), **true blue** (unshakeably loyal to established social values), and **a true friend** (in time of need, etc.).

The distinction between these two kinds of truth has greatly widened in recent years, for two main reasons. The first is that the body of critically-established, academically-approved objective truth is now very large, and much or most of it is expressed in very unfamiliar technical vocabularies. It has become *expert truth*, dispensed to us by experts who represent the whole professional group to which they belong,. They give their testimony in a specially cool, careful and impersonal tone of voice that reminds us that they are choosing their words with great care, and are speaking with a special kind of judicial impartiality. They are acting as *advisors*.

At such a moment the register of the conversation changes abruptly and very strikingly. The play of forces that we call life pauses while the expert speaks; for what the expert says, though a locution, is not an illocution, nor is it a perlocution. It makes no contribution to life: it is not a part of life. It doesn't have that kind of *force*. It enters the scene from a point outside life, and (supposedly) acts as a valuable reminder. Then, when the expert has said his piece and we have digested his remarks, then the ordinary hubbub of life resumes, the conversation continues—and we sometimes wonder how we can be sure whether or not the players have fully taken in what the expert has just said.

Now take a look at the texts of a number of plays by some major writer such as Beckett or Pinter. See how they depict the to and fro of conversational exchange. Blows are traded, connections are or are not being made, silences are eloquent, bombshells are dropped, feelings are expressed . . . and to all this play and counterplay just how much contribution is made by critical thinking and critically-tested knowledge? Apparently, none whatever. During the past few centuries critical thinking and critically-established knowledge have developed enormously and have become the basis of a very wide range of new technologies. The frame within which our life is set has changed considerably—but life itself continues with little change. Theoretical knowledge, it seems, makes little difference to life. Yes, the critically-established *expert* kind of truth is indeed invoked now and again in certain special situations. Life pauses for a while: people digest what they are hearing, and then we may become aware as life resumes that the power-relations between the speakers have shifted a little. But that is it. We may add that in modern developed societies many or most workers have to familiarize themselves with the small portion of the great stock of critically-established knowledge that they require in order to do their jobs adequately. Remember, for example, that Homer Simpson works in the control room of a nuclear power plant. But as ordinary usage reminds us, 'work' is not part of 'life', and the (very modest) bit of technical expertise that Homer must use to do his job does not have any detectable effect on the way he thinks and speaks in his real life. Perhaps this is why governments see universities merely as places where students are taught employable skills. I hate to say it, but they could be right.

All of which goes to show that in modern times knowledge and truth have come down in the world considerably. They have grown so huge that they are distributed amongst tens of thousands of distinct specialist occupations, and nobody knows it all, or is even interested in doing so. The former very high valuation of knowledge belonged to an epoch when philosophy was the contemplation of a higher world of eternal verities. People held a realist view of truth, such as is implied by phrases like **seekers after truth** and **the truth is out there**. The world was not merely brute fact: it existed as held within God's absolute knowledge of it. There was truth out there, because there were answers to all questions out there in the mind of God. It was obvious that you needed to achieve a clear and intuitive knowledge of how things are in the eternal world before you could hope to live well, and in the end achieve eternal happiness. For religious people this meant that life's ultimate goal was the visionary knowledge of God, and that in the shorter term it was vital that you should hold the correct dogmatic beliefs about God and the supernatural world. Knowledge came first, and religion was about God and the eternal world. Truth was, above all, eternal and blessedness-giving Truth.

However, since the French Revolution the focus of interest in philosophy and in religious thought has been steadily shifting, from the Intelligible World Above to this present world, and from God to life. In the process the old kind of absolute knowledge has been replaced by the typically-modern development of a huge body of critically-established *expert* knowledge; but this newer kind of knowledge, though it has in many ways considerably *eased* life (we live longer, life's less laborious), makes surprisingly little difference to the actual living of life.

This leads me to the second corollary of the expert truth/moral truth distinction from which I began. As we have become more aware of the play of language in everyday life, so we have come to see that in ordinary life language is customarily used not judiciously to inform, but persuasively in order to advance people's positions in the various power-games that they are playing. Moral truth is the trustworthiness and the reliability of that which we can and should rely upon in our daily battles with the opposite sex, with the next generation, and with our colleagues. (That's in order of importance and general bloodiness.) Life is micropolitics, and moral truth is what you can trust 'implicitly', or without having to think about it, in the hurly-burly of daily life.

Here the complication arises that modern liberal democratic societies are very plural, politically, morally, religiously. People have a great variety of different allegiances, ethnic, religious, generational, and so on, and the moral kind of truth has become highly segmented. What's worse, the critical style of thinking and the wide range of methods of truth-testing that it has developed seem to be unable to do anything to resolve the chronic conflicts between different moral truths that plague modern societies. It is true that after 200 years or so critical thinking has had some *internal* effect within Christianity (amongst theologians and intellectuals), within Judaism, and even, in a very small way, within Islam. There has as a result been a significant weakening of the strength of faith within each of these great religions. But the main body or bodies of believers within each tradition remain obdurately pre-critical in outlook. They take no notice whatever of the modern critical-academic way to truth. It may (just) do a little to improve their understanding of each other's claims and values, but it cannot help at all to negotiate their confessional disagreements. Religious and moral truth, it seems, are purely political, which is why opinions about them are always described not in intellectual terms but as being *conservative*, *liberal* or *radical*, as being *extremist* or *moderate*, and as being *strict* or *lax*. The entire field of moral truth is about clusters of values that shape our life-policies, and about kinds and degrees of loyalty. It is not about different accounts of what works, or what is the case. Accordingly the leaders of society nowadays should be followers of Niccolo Machiavelli and Thomas Hobbes. All religions, ethnicities, political parties and so on should be treated as non-rational forces, and should be shrewdly managed by the wise statesman so that they do not cause violent social disruption or upheaval.

The statesman or stateswoman cannot wholly avoid paradoxes. Multicultural states may try to define a broad and spreading civil umbrella beneath which a great variety of different ethnicities and faith groups can coexist peacefully, but some groups are notoriously hard to satisfy and persistently test the limits of toleration. But if we are obliged to admit that many religious conflicts are not rationally negotiable, it would seem that political leaders have no choice but to be followers of Hobbes and Macchiavelli in the short run, while hoping in the long run quietly to manage the most inassimilable groups out of existence. I think it will be possible to do this eventually, provided that the state does all it can to cultivate a single common language and popular culture.

What of people like me, and perhaps also you—people for whom it is personally important that we have religious freedom in a free society, without having to endure chronic religious conflict? We want true religion to live by, religion that is entirely sociable and peaceful, and that is on principle *not* provocative. So:

1. We recognize that we must give up the dogmatic side of religion, which notoriously makes untestable claims about a supernatural world, about gods and spirits etc.

2. We give up objective truth, and limit ourselves to testable, pragmatic truth, *expert* truth—truth as what works or can be made to work—and *moral* truth, which is truth that can be lived by and done.

3. We admit that a religion must now be seen simply as a way of relating oneself to life, and as a cluster of values that shape living.

4. Our religion takes the new form of an immediate, beliefless and 'solar' commitment to life itself, as we live it. This solar living seeks to be as purely-affirmative as possible, without making any movement of rejection and condemnation. It seeks to revalue the human world—or at least to revalue its own corner of the world. Its social ethic is simply humanitarian, because our common humanity is the only common and objective basis for ethics that is left to us.

And that is true religion, now. It is solar living, as purely affirmative and expressive as it knows how to be. As for knowledge and truth, Nietzsche was right: they are less important now than we used to think. Under Platonism, knowledge of eternal truth in a better world was the only way to blessedness. But now life is all we have, and it is what matters most of all. 'Life, life!', as the fleeing man cries in *The Pilgrim's Progress*.

4

REALITY, AFTER THE END
OF METAPHYSICS

One of our deepest and most tenaciously-held assumptions is the assumption that we have come into being, and we now find ourselves set, within a readymade world, orderly, fully-formed and already running like clockwork. A system of *physical* or natural laws, and also of natural *moral* law, is already operational. It is all in place, ready for us, and just sitting there, waiting for us to come along and understand it—as we can. Amazing.

We believe all this chiefly because it is what our culture's traditional Creation-myth seems to be telling us. Indeed, it is what our theologians actually *believed* until barely two centuries ago. Such a fully-formed world, already in motion autonomously and independently of us, is in Greek called a Cosmos. For Christians, the power of God guaranteed the objective reality of the Cosmos, and the wisdom of God its order. But before Christianity the Greeks had already raised the question of how the Notself around us, the stage on which we live, apparently contrives to be a complete, fully-formed, sweetly-running world, all just *there*, without any contribution on our part. How can this be? Plato's popular answer—in the *Timaeus*—makes a distinction between the *matter* of the world, visible and unstable stuff, and the *form* of the world, the general intellectual principles by which the world is ordered (and which of course are *not* visible). Then Plato tells a story about a world-architect who makes the Cosmos we have by imposing the intellectual principles—general kinds, natural laws, etc.—upon the world's matter. Thus Plato has a creator of sorts, even before Christianity. But Plato's Creator is only a finite world-architect, who has one eye upon the world of eternal Forms and takes from it the patterns and rules he follows in shaping the raw material of the world. The later Christian Creator is far grander. The whole intellectual world of the Forms is comprised within his mind, and his almighty power creates the whole matter of the world out of nothing, so that he is the absolute Creator of the cosmos and it can be seen as his living art-work, and an expression of his mind.

Thus in our tradition the belief that we have around us a ready-made, fully-formed and sweetly-running world became eventually (in 1215 C.E., in fact!) a *purely theological* belief, affirmed in the Creed. The world is real because God has made it so, for us.

It follows, strictly, that when people lose belief in God, they should also lose belief in the cosmos. Atheists must be a-cosmists, too. But this didn't happen. God died soon after Newton, whose celestial mechanics was most carefully and minutely recalculated by Pierre Simon, Marquis de Laplace (1749–1827). Laplace finally and definitively cleared up various anomalies, and proved Newtonianism right. As for God, Laplace famously declared—or is said to have declared—'I have no need of that hypothesis'. But in that case, why did Laplace go on believing in the existence of the Cosmos, God's creation? Equally extraordinary, how was Laplace to account for the weird fact that his own animal brain, although no longer made in the image of the Creator, remained so prodigiously good at tracking the Cosmic order?

The question is still puzzling to this day, and Darwinism has made it even more perplexing. Why are so many scientists still firmly attached to a realist and highly theological view of the world, and also of themselves and their own mentality? They believe in an objectively existing world out there, in an objective and intelligible world-order, and in the human mind's innate and preformed aptitude for tracking the same world-order (with the aid, nowadays, of a lot of very fancy maths). But how do people go *on* holding these theological beliefs, after God?

Some answers can be conjectured. For example, it has generally been held that the world is purely contingent. It is not held in being by any logical necessity: it merely happens to be. But what keeps it in being, if it is not upheld from moment to moment by the creative Will of God? Perhaps in reply to this scientists will fall back upon the ancient idea, held by some of the Greeks, of the eternity of matter—merely updating it, and renaming it 'the conservation of matter/energy'.

Very well. Now, another question: if there is no lawgiver, what *are* the 'laws of nature', and what constrains the world-stuff to obey them, everywhere and even under the most extreme conditions? Perhaps at this point people will want to invoke something called 'the Uniformity of Nature'. But many theorists question that today.

For years I have been haunted by a third puzzle: What *regulates* the process of the world? If a clock's escapement mechanism becomes disengaged, it will accelerate crazily until it crashes when the mainspring becomes fully unwound. Why doesn't the world-process accelerate out of control and crash in that way? What *paces* the world? In prescientific thought the gods were careful to set our minds at rest on this point. They were very keen regulators, who guaranteed by covenant the stability of all the natural rhythms within which we live. But now?

These three examples illustrate the general rule that we can't live in just any old world. Pure chaos, for example, would drive us mad instantly. To be habitable by us, and to make sense to us, the world has to be ordered in various ways. Very roughly, it needs to be spread out in space and time, its matter needs to be conserved, its motions law-abiding, and its major rhythms regular. (This is an absolutely minimal specification: if we took the time to work it all out, we'd soon see that a good deal more than that is needed.)

Now in the days when people believed in gods, they supposed that the gods in their wisdom had taken pains to ensure that they created for us a world fit to live in. but what happens now, after the gods have fled and all we have left is the scientific world-picture? Who or what ensures the general habitability and intelligibility of the world?

The question is particularly awkward, because we humans never actually *see* space or time or the most general principles of natural philosphy directly. All we actually have to go on is the mass of data that is coming in all the time through our sense organs. Spits and spots of sensation: how does it all get built into the coherent and objective world we actually have around us?

At this point I have to refer to the greatest event in the history of Western philosophy, namely the publication of Immanuel Kant's *Critique of Pure Reason* in 1781. He is still asking the old question: How does chaos get formed into an orderly, habitable cosmos? But instead of repeating an old creation myth about how the gods did it all at the beginning of time, he tells a new story about how *we* do it, all the time. The framework principles for a habitable objective world are already there, in our own understanding, like a kind of permanent programming. They seize upon, interpret, and file the incoming data of experience, so that sense-experience gets formed into knowledge of an objective world, and Chaos becomes Cosmos. Thus *we* make the world make sense.

Kant draws attention to an important corollary of his view of knowledge. It always involves a synthesis of two things, which he terms 'concepts' and 'intuitions'. By concepts he means the general ideas and rules that are immanent within the human understanding, and by intuitions he means simply the raw data of experience. All knowledge involves the mind's interpretation of experience. It follows that our knowledge can never pretend altogether to outsoar the world of experience, which in turn means that 'dogmatic metaphysics' is dead; and that all our knowledge involves interpretation, which in turn means that we have no absolute knowledge of things as they are in themselves.

So we have only *our world*. We can never have *the world*, absolutely or 'perspectivelessly', and we can never go beyond the world. Kant cannot strictly prove the objective reality of our world, but he does argue that we must build our world as we do and must think of it as objective, if we are to have a world at all. But we *do* have a world, we can show philosophically that we *must* build it the way we do—and that's all there is to say.

From Kant stems the great tradition of German Idealist philosophy. Here we do not need to do more than quote what had happened to Kant's themes a century later, in the (post-darwinian) thought of the young Nietzsche. The slogans are familiar:

God is dead.

There are no facts, only interpretations.

Our truths are those illusions without which we cannot live.

As for the end of metaphysics, I guess Heidegger was right in saying that we see it happening most clearly and explicitly in the thought of the young Marx, around 1840. Here we need to say a little about the history of objective reality.

As we have seen, classical Western monotheism, with its very strong ideas of God's infinite power and wisdom, gave us a very strong sense of the reality of the created world, of its suitability to be our home, and of the ability of our own minds both to understand the world-order, and to commune with the God who had made it for us, and us for himself. Classical theism was always *predestinarian*: every event in world-history was foreordained by God, and therefore had to happen as it did. There was no cloud of other, unfulfilled possibilities hanging over events. There was only what God had willed, which would certainly happen, and what God had *not* willed, which was impossible. All this conveyed to people a very strong sense of reality.

Then in the seventeenth century everything began to change. René Descartes was trying to develop a philosophical rationale for the new and purely manmade mathematical physics. The physicist sets out his definitions of matter, motion, space and time, then his laws of motion, and then his formulae for making calculations. But when he has developed his system of mathematical physics—a system of ideas—how is he to prove that there is a Real World out there of which the system is true and to which it applies? Suddenly Descartes sees that the new science has a problem: whence do all its ideas get their 'objective reality'? Descartes seems to have been the first person to use this new phrase. He is puzzled—and he falls back upon God. God's power and his veracity guarantee to us the objective reality of the physical world.

Fine, but here as everywhere else Descartes eventually finds himself starting more doubts than he is securing certainties. Just after his time the mathematics of statistical probability develops. People start to think of the course of coming events as a matter of science-based predictions and projections; as a matter of calculable probabilities, rather than theological certainties. They start wondering why, out of all the innumerable possible worlds, just *this* one should happen to be actual. And, indeed, what *is* its 'happening to be actual'?

Here is an irony: 'objective reality' began to melt away almost as soon as Descartes became aware of the need for it, and invented it. Strong realism has never been restored. Since Nietzsche there have been two main currents in philosophy: one has been getting more and more sceptical (for example, French 'poststructuralism'), and one (for example, Wittgenstein) that looks for ways of persuading us not to fret so much about our lost 'absolutes'. I guess that the chief reason why thoroughgoing Islamists despise us Westerners so much is that from their point of view we have irretrievably lost all sense of real, objective existence and value. The only way of escape for us is by their total victory over us. They alone can give us back the objective God and the objective values that we miss so much. So if you are a Western religious conservative, you must welcome the forthcoming Islamist victory over the West. It will deliver you—or at least, it promises to deliver you—from the 'relativism' you hate, and it will give you back the 'absolutes' you crave.

Alternatively, if you think that the journey of the West from Descartes to Derrida and Baudrillard is irreversible now, then you must give up worrying about objective reality, give up dogmatic religious belief, and start practising solar ethics, the religion of ordinary life, and the remaking of the world as art.

Which path will you take?

5

LANGUAGE AND ITS OUTSIDELESSNESS

In the long period dominated by Plato (roughly, from 350 BCE to 1800 CE), when there was a sharp distinction between the sensuous world below and the eternal, purely intelligible world above, it was usually thought that whereas science is concerned with the lower world of the senses and empirical fact, philosophy is concerned with the higher world of *a priori*, eternal truth. To do philosophy, you raised your sights. A modern version of that old doctrine would have to say something rather different, like this: in philosophy many of the toughest and most interesting questions have to do with matters that are very hard to get a hold of because we are so deeply immersed in them all the time. We can't distance ourselves from them so as to get a cool, detached and 'scientific' view of them. Examples are *time*, *being*, *consciousness* and *language*. Philosophy is nowadays very often not about things that are too high up and far off for us, but about things that are always presupposed, too close to us, so that we can't easily get them into focus. To find philosophy's space, don't climb *up*: step *back*.

In the Middle Ages the wandering planets sang as they circled in their orbits, their songs adding up to a most beautiful chord, the music of the spheres. But we human beings were unable to hear this cosmic harmony, because it sounded so evenly all the time. Similarly, it is very hard indeed to state the so-called 'problem of consciousness' accurately, because we are always in it. It is always already there, always presupposed. It is the very air we breathe: it is our life. You never know that you're not conscious, and you never will know it: the mind 'always thinks', as Descartes remarks. The mind cannot find any place outside consciousness. Consciousness has no outside; it encompasses everything.

I am suggesting that time, be-ing (i.e. temporal existence), consciousness and language are all of them things that are always already there, always presupposed, outsideless and impossible to jump out of. But the precise point being made here is curiously difficult to grasp, and many of humankind's most tempting and persistent illusions are generated by our failure to understand and accept the truth of outsidelessness. Of such illusions, the dream of a *totum simul* (all at once) is the worst. It is the dream that we can jump clear of language and temporal succession and achieve an immediate, total, all-at-once, 'intuitive' visionary communion with the object of our desire. I don't think anyone has quite noticed this before (unless it can be found somewhere in late Derrida) but the mistake is very much the same whether it be made by human lovers, by religious faith, or by rationalist philosophers. Perhaps we should add: or even by revolutionary political utopians. Our desire is urgent. We can't wait. We want to achieve the supreme goal quickly, and we want it all at once. Ordinarily, we can't do this because the fact that we are finite, temporal beings means that we can only scan or experience a great and complex object *seriatim*, a bit at a time, in such a way that by the time we get to the end of the series the beginning has long since slipped away. That's the law of life. *You can't have it all at once*; and our modern awareness of our linguisticality makes matters even worse. We long to jump clear of language and to commune immediately with the object of our faith, or our love, or our intellectual passion. Hence the old contrast between a *discursive* and an *intuitive* understanding. But the thing that we so much desire we just cannot have. You can have more-or-less anything, provided only that you understand and accept that *you can have it only language-wrapped*—that is, mediated by language's secondary, symbolic and always-ambiguous quality. If you have dreamt of a pure, living, reciprocal Presence to each other of you and your beloved, or of you and your god, or of the rational necessity that you are trying to prove and to comprehend; if you are dreaming of that sort of consummation, forget it. You can't have it all at once. You can have it *only* piecemeal, a bit of a time, and never quite unambiguously.

Do not misunderstand me. I am not saying that we are *stuck* in discursiveness, and can never rise to the level of pure intuition: I am not saying that we are *stuck* in time and can never rise to the level of eternity; and I am not saying that we are *isolated* selves that can never really give ourselves completely to the Other. I am saying rather that we simply *are* our own secondariness, our own linguisticality, our own temporality, and our own irresolvable ambiguities. There never was and there never will be any other option for us, so we are not really missing anything. We are not imprisoned in a lower world: we are simply what we are. I am not trying to take away from you anything that you could have, something that in the ages of faith was readily available to all. No, the *totum simul* was always an illusion, but they did not know it.

The history of critical thinking in our tradition—Socrates, Descartes, Kant, Nietzsche, Derrida—has been the history of a long process of dis-illusionment, recently completed in the appropriately difficult and irritating work of Derrida. Perhaps, too, we should see the message of Wittgenstein as having been essentially the same. Somehow we human beings have always—or at least, we have for as far back as we can trace—found ourselves quite unable simply to accept that our life is neither more nor less than just what it is. We have assiduously cultivated dreams of a better world with more solid joys and lasting treasures. Reason, faith, human love, and social hope have all sought to overcome the limits of life and achieve the perfect *totum simul* that they dreamt of. It is very hard indeed to persuade human beings to give up these ancient illusory hopes, and simply accept and celebrate our ordinary life. But now we no longer have any excuse. The religious challenge now is not to find some way of patching up the old hopes and keeping them going in reduced form for just a little longer, but to learn to say a wholehearted religious Yes to life as it is, and as a package deal. As Nietzsche says: 'With the real world we have also abolished the apparent world!' When we have finally got rid of platonism, we no longer think of what is left in terms of either reality or appearance. It simply is what it is: it is 'life'. Which is no doubt why a recent post-Derrida volume was given the title *Life.After.Theory*.[5] After the fireworks and the smoke caused by the irruption of post-structuralist ideas during the late 1960s, and then after decades of debate about 'theory', the smoke clears and what is left is simply 'life'.

The point has been made easier to grasp by our gradually clearer recognition of the nature of our living vernacular languages. For centuries Western scholars studied only various dead languages, with the help of formalized grammar-books and dictionaries. The classical language was laid out cold on a slab for study. The way a living language gradually evolves historically, the way the meanings of words shift continuously, and the way language functions as the currency of all our social life, much as money functions as the currency of our economic life—all this was simply not seen clearly. But as the Enlightenment passed over into the Romantic Movement in writers from Rousseau and Herder to Schiller and von Humboldt, something like a modern understanding of language began to develop. People began to think about the relations between the language of myth and poetry, the language of philosophy, and the language of everyday life. The old idea that we think in pure concepts like the angels[6] began to give way to the newer idea that thinking is just internalized speech (*innerliche Sprache*): we may indeed have some capacity to entertain simple images non-linguistically, but all meaningful, connected, propositional thought is simply a shadowy, half-completed motion of natural language in our heads.

Everything else now follows—not just that our world is always language-wrapped, and mediated to us in and by our language, but much more; namely that the living motion of our language, around the English-speaking world every day, not merely *builds* our life-world, but *is* our life-world. It's not just that everything in our world is copied in our language in minute detail, but that our living language *is* the world in which we think, and act, and are ourselves. As in the play *Hamlet* what Hamlet is is given in the text by all the things that are said by Hamlet, and to a lesser extent to him and about him by others; so we ourselves, what we *are*, is given by the language used by us, and to a lesser extent to us and about us. We just are our lived lives in our life-world, and our life is lived within our living, moving language. You are what you say: you are your part in life.

Our language is then radically human, radically *ours*, and radically *itself* our human life-world, rich, but unbounded. The more deeply we come to understand what our language is, what we are, and what our world is, the more deeply we must take in the truth of 'outsidelessness', or radical immanence. Life, our life, our language, is all there is. That is why any story about some non-human being—whether it be a god, or an alien, a spirit, or an animal—talking human language can only be a story about a human being dressed up. If it talks a human language, it has to be a human being. In retrospect it is quite amazing that so many of the world's greatest religions were founded in epochs when humans had never paid any serious attention to their own language and therefore freely committed the preposterous howler of claiming that the eternal God composed the scriptures in our language in his own mind before the world was created, and then caused them to be dictated by an angel to a human scribe. In their haste, those faiths describe their scriptures as 'the Word of God', as if they had never noticed that language is radically temporal, whereas their God was supposed by definition to be eternal. A sentence's meaning depends upon the word-order within it, and the end of a sentence has to be delivered later—*temporally* later—than its beginning. So how can an eternal being, who can know nothing of temporal experience, think in or utter a human language? People who thought, and indeed *still* think, in such ways have clearly not yet begun to consider what their own language is. They haven't noticed that language is social, human, set in time and space, gendered and so on. So they still picture God as a language-using being like themselves. It's fantasy. It always was, and it still is.

Just language itself, then, forces the move we must now make to a purely human, this-worldly religion of ordinary life. It does not allow the possibility of any other world or any other life than this. Our language allows us only one life in only one world: everything else, we should now forget forever.

It is necessary to close this section with some remarks about the very common amateurish belief that it is possible, perhaps in the silence of word-less prayer, for the human mind wordlessly to grope after and to intuit the objective reality of God, real out there and beyond the mind. Since it has been generally conceded that the classic arguments for the existence of God do not succeed, a great number of ordinary realistic theists (perhaps even the majority of them) have fallen back on a claim of this kind, as offering a somewhat-shadowy experimental verification of their belief in God. They hold a pre-Wittgensteinian 'copying' view of linguistic representation; that is, they think they can use language to conjure up a great dark ineffable region beyond language in which they can 'sense' or 'feel' the presence of God as they pray.

Perplexed, I ask what sort of sensing or feeling is this, and how can you tell that it's a feeling *of God*? How, I ask, can one have a *hunch* of objective existence beyond the mind? It sounds extremely vague and muddled, but it evidently matters a great deal to people, for they go on saying: 'There must be something there, something in it'. They are evidently clinging to something that is very important to them, but perhaps they have not yet realized how impossibly paradoxical all talk about an ineffable silent realm beyond language is.

A Buddhist story repeated by Paul Reps has a great host of monks assembled in a vast heavenly amphitheatre for a long debate. One monk stands to deliver a homily about the Buddhist version of the supreme good: 'No words are adequate to speak of it', he says, 'It is beyond speech, it is even beyond all thought', and so on, and on. Then the next speaker gets up to address the mighty throng. 'Did the last speaker say anything?' he asks.

6

LIFE, AND MY LIFE

In and around the year 1998 I was debating with myself whether to rebuild my philosophy around the word Being, or around the word Life. I was just emerging from two short books in which I had been wrestling with Heidegger's notion of Being.[7] Was it to be written ~~Being~~, by way of marking it as a non-word for something that is prior to language and in principle elusive? Or would it be better to write it 'Be-ing', by way of making the point that in our modern, historically-minded epoch there is no timeless, absolute Being? All existence is flowing and transient: it pours out silently, and it passes away. Or perhaps I would do better to take up Heidegger's term 'Dasein', being-there, and use a word that would highlight our own human and historically-situated kind of existence?

I was ruminating about these matters at a time when many of us were beginning to take stock after a twenty-year flurry of excitement over catching up with modern Continental philosophy in general, and with French structuralist and post-structuralist thought in particular. Theory, it was often called, critical theory. The great generation were already beginning to disappear, and as we all came down to earth we were wondering what permanent difference it had made to us. Where next?

It was at this juncture that I took up another project, the idea of trying to discover the ordinary person's philosophy by collecting and interpreting all the relevant idioms in ordinary language—the sayings that people fall back upon when they are trying to articulate their sense of **what it's all about**. I had collected over a hundred very striking idioms that used the word **life**, and was beginning to write about them. Soon it became clear to me that in ordinary language a very large-scale shift of attention from God to Life had already taken place during the two generations since the Second World War. Language itself, apparently, had already answered my question for me, and we are all of us moving over—largely unawares—to a new religion of ordinary life. The 1960s had marked the end of the old tradition-directed kind of society in which ordinary people **looked up** for religious and moral guidance. They had looked up in the past to the supernatural world, to the upper social classes, to the older generation, and to tradition generally. But now they suddenly realized that they no longer felt any need to look up in that way. Consider the idioms in which ordinary people now talk about how they plan to get back to normality, after their lives have been violently disrupted by a major trauma. They say:

> I'm thinking of moving away and trying to rebuild my life . . .
>
> All I want now is to get back to living my own ordinary life . . .
>
> Starting a new life . . .
>
> I want my life back . . .

It seems that an age has arrived in which ordinary people ask no more of life than the freedom to assume full responsibility for their own lives, so that they can live out their own ordinary lives in their own way. This new democratized and secular understanding of human existence first begins to appear in seventeenth-century Dutch Protestantism, and then progressively takes over after the French Revolution. It is often reaffirmed in the popular novel, and in French Impressionist painting. Vincent Van Gogh discusses it very well in his letters,[8] and the American patrons who bought Paris-School art in such quantities clearly recognized a close affinity between American optimism and the new European sense of the innocent ordinariness of modern urban life.

The philosophers have used a surprising variety of terms to express their sense of the new post-metaphysical world-picture. The basic idea is that instead of seeing everything as grounded in a timeless God or in the metaphysical order, we should see everything as grounded in a flowing process of historical development; a process of individual and social expression and exchange which now has to be seen as the matrix out of which everything, but *everything*, emerges.

What then is the great developing process of exchange to be called? Spirit, or Geist, says Hegel. History, read in dialectical materialist terms, says Marx. Life, say some of the post-darwinian vitalists. Husserl talks of the life-world, and Heidegger of the history of Being, and of Dasein.

I want to say **life**, partly because it is the term that our ordinary language has already chosen, and partly because my Darwin-and-Freud background (not to mention a good deal of personal experience) has made me aware of the extent to which the whole process of human existence is fuelled and driven by the emotions, continually pouring out and seeking expression. Life is the whole flowing developing world of human existence, social, cultural, historical; it is the ceaseless noisy conversation of human-ity, which we now see to be the universal matrix or seedbed out of which everything else grows.

As Pierre says in *War and Peace*: 'Life is God, and to love life is to love God'. Especially in post-1962 experience, **Life** has now largely or entirely taken the place of God.

The first thing to be differentiated out of life is **my life**. My life is the bit of the whole stream of life that I need to claim and to own as mine. I need to find my own best way of living my own life, and of living it to the full, so that I can contribute something to the whole.

At this point it is very convenient to compare the new religion with the old. **My life** is the modern counterpart of what used to be called 'my soul'. John Calvin, at the beginning of his *Institutes of the Christian Religion*, and John Henry Newman, at the beginning of his *Apologia pro Vita Sua*, have very eloquent and very similar passages about how from a religious point of view our greatest and most fundamental concern has to be with the relation of the soul to God. God and the Soul, the two supreme realities, they both say. I am replacing their doctrine with the truth of our own contemporary experience, which is that before all else I must appropriate and claim my own life—and therewith my own inalienable duty to make something of it. Just as in the old days I must not 'sell my soul', so today I mustn't allow anyone else to take for me the basic decisions that will shape my future life. I must make my own small contribution, I must **do my bit**. Above all, I need for the sake of everyone to find some way of being 'solar' (joyous, expressive, affirmative, outgoing) in the face of the limits and the dark side of life. Manifest solar joy in life is the modern replacement for the old idea of 'sainthood', which is now very, very dead.

One further piece of replacement vocabulary before we move on. Although everyone today admires the love of life and the capacity for joy in life, we are also acutely aware of the constant threat posed by the limits of life—traditionally, temporality, contingency and finitude. Many, many lives are appallingly blighted by poverty, violence, chronic and terminal ill-ness, and other personal disasters. It seems clear that the traditional 'sense of sin' and the doctrine of 'Original Sin' have today been replaced by our awareness of the very high proportion of all lives that are blighted.

Two main lines of response stand out. One is the long, steady growth of 'humanitarian' concern for human suffering since the mid and late eigh-teenth century. It is expressed in the foundation of a very wide range of movements such as the Anti-Slavery Society (1785) and the International Committee of the Red Cross (1853). Think how, even as late as Waterloo, the wounded and the dead were simply left on the battlefield, to be stripped of their clothing and teeth by scavengers from nearby towns. Even the most savage of us are no longer as inhumane as *that*.

Secondly, we have come to see faith as the courage to live, say Yes to life, and find solar joy in life despite everything. That is our modern equivalent of the traditional 'joy in affliction'. It leads me to conclude that a new religion of commitment simply to one's own life is already quietly establishing itself all around the world. It does not need any professional apologists, nor any visible organization of its own. It is simply what we are all of us coming to believe. So I'm not telling you what I think; I'm just helping you to get a bit clearer about what you are already coming to think.

7

THE LIMITS OF LIFE

Plato and standard Christian doctrine underlie the way tradition has taught us to see what in recent years I have been calling 'the limits of life'.

Plato's texts established in the Western tradition a number of sharp binary oppositions that he had introduced in setting up his great contrast between the invisible and visible worlds. The world above was *eternal*, and the world below was *temporal*. The higher, noumenal realm was a world of *necessary* truth, whereas the unstable phenomenal world below was a world of merely-short-term and *contingent* truths—if indeed there was anything at all in the lower world that really deserved to be called truth. Everything in the upper world was flawlessly *perfect* and standard-setting, whereas everything in the lower world was unstable and *imperfect*. The world above was a world of unchangeable *Being*, and the lower world was a world of everchanging *Becoming*. And so on: the one great contrast that is familiar to us but which is not actually in Plato's text is the *infinite/finite* contrast. It is in his spirit, but it was added only in late antiquity, when there was a great desire to stress God's infinity.

In Christian doctrine, then, the contrast between the two worlds became a contrast between the Creator and the creature. God was accorded the 'metaphysical attributes' of eternity, necessity and infinity, with the obvious corollary that every creature was to be described as being temporal, contingent and finite. Inevitably, God's creature had to fall short of God's own perfection. Apologists were apt to picture the creature as being God's polar opposite, and therefore as being almost *necessarily* imperfect, and this sort-of-necessary imperfection of the creature came in Leibniz's philosophy to be descried as 'metaphysical evil'. The axiom was that whatever is made must be relatively imperfect compared with its maker.

It is worth mentioning here that Leibniz is one of the very few great Western philosophers to have written a treatise on what is usually called 'the Problem of Evil'. In his *Theodicée* (=the justification of God), published in 1710, Leibniz distinguishes three main kinds of evil that afflict us humans: he uses the term 'moral evil' to describe the human sinfulness and wickedness that result from the misuse of our (or Adam's) freedom of will; he uses the term 'natural evil' to describe the physical pain and suffering to which humans and other animals are liable in a world of bodies in motion, a world of occasional natural disasters, accidents and disease; and he reserves the term 'metaphysical evil' for the consequences of the fact that we creatures cannot help but fall short of God's own unlimited power, perfection and life. (Note here a technical point: the gap between the finite and the Infinite is *itself* infinite, so that strictly speaking the finite creature must fall *infinitely* short of the Creator's divine perfection.)

Leibniz was almost the last important philosopher to write a big book of basic theology that was (more or less) fully compatible with Christian orthodoxy. Very soon after him came the metaphysical 'Death of God', and philosophy began to look for alternatives to the old platonic vocabulary. But, surprisingly, after the Death of God the world was not at once revalued. Perhaps there was a desire to reassure people, by persuading them that the world was still in place, and things had not changed very much. At any rate, in many quarters Nature continued to be thought of—and spoken of—as 'Creation', and it continued to be thought of as being somehow 'inevitably' imperfect—not least (as we have seen) because, once the Creator had been defined as 'infinitely' perfect, it followed that the creature fell infinitely short of God's perfection.

In parenthesis, Protestant theology, especially in the Reformed tradition of Calvinism, tended to disapprove of mediaeval philosophy and tried as far as it could to speak of God and the world in non-philosophical language. Thus in John Milton's ode 'On Time', temporality, contingency and finitude, Leibniz's metaphysical evil, appear as Time, Chance and Death. These ancient, devouring enemies still rampage through the world, but faith looks forward to seeing them destroyed one day.

On the whole, then, and with only rare exceptions, we can conclude that *both* in the Catholic and philosophical tradition of Plato, the 'schoolmen' and Leibniz, *and* in the Reformed tradition of Calvin and Milton, the world we live in has tended to emerge from the Christian centuries *blighted*. Its transience, its imperfection, its liability to inflict sudden personal catastrophe upon us, and its dangers as a place of temptation have continued to be emphasized. Extreme dread of the passage of time, as dragging us daily closer to death and divine Judgement, has not merely *survived* the death of God but in some ways has actually been *exacerbated* by it. That seems very illogical: Dr Samuel Johnson feared death because he feared the awesome judgment that he thought would follow it, but why should gloomy post-Christians from Schopenhauer to Philip Larkin, who certainly did not expect judgement nor feared damnation, continue to fear death so much as they did? They had nothing to fear—and yet they were absolutely terrified.

There are a few early examples of post-Christian unbelievers who either were (or managed to become) of a sunny and easy-going disposition, and were able to approach death without fear. David Hume is a well-known example. But the very fact that so many of his contemporaries found Hume's cheerful unbelief shocking, and even went like Boswell to visit him on his deathbed in the hope of finding him as apprehensive as they considered he should be, rather shows that amongst the orthodox a gloomy and pessimistic view of life and its limits remained pretty much as it always had been. Hence Nietzsche's verdict: God had first sucked all the value out of life—and then God died, leaving the world devalued. How extraordinary that the religion of the Incarnation, whose whole message had been about the *return* of divinity into the world and into human life, should end up by achieving the exact opposite of its own express aim!

An even more curious and painful illustration of the same point is this: that although Christianity can with some pride point to the fact that it has on the whole been less actively malignant to women than any other major world faith—well, a *little* less malignant—nevertheless to this day female sexuality and the female reproductive system remain somewhat blighted even in Christian cultures—in spite of the claim that the Son of God 'did not abhor the Virgin's womb'! The standard Christian doctrine that ought to have sanctified femaleness seems to have left a moral legacy the exact opposite of what it professed.

Two simple illustrations of the problem. In most or all major religious traditions a woman menstruating is seen as being in a condition of ritual impurity. It is ordered that she should not enter a holy place or house of prayer in that condition, and very often that she must perform some ritual of purification such as bathing.

In Christianity the main body of official teaching seems always to have allowed a menstruating woman to attend Church, and to receive communion. Pope St Gregory I says so, in one of the most decent and humane of all papal pronouncements. But sexual intercourse with a menstruating woman remained the subject of strong disapproval almost up to modern times, and I find that even the most modern Dictionaries of English and of Slang still record the use (by women themselves, mainly) of the expression 'the curse'—short for 'the curse of Eve'. That expression strongly suggests to me that many women themselves still feel that their whole sex is blighted.

The second illustration has to do with female sexual display. Around the world, and I think in all or most major religious traditions, devout men tend to regard female display—which usually involves much attention to cosmetics, hairdressing, clothes and (perhaps most of all) the purchase of highly uncomfortable shoes—with deep anger and disapproval. Women are often kept in seclusion and allowed out in public only when heavily veiled.

As a young person, I was lucky in that I spent my last three years at school and my first two years at university largely in the study of biology; and, broadly speaking, biology teaches you sane and wholesome attitudes to sexual matters, whereas all established religions have detestable views about sex. So I learnt that there is no reason whatever to regard sexual display, in either sex, as being anything else but entirely natural and rather charming. It is an expression of *joie de vivre*. So we may be tempted to congratulate ourselves, and to say rather smugly that at least Christian cultures are not quite as savagely repressive and inhuman as Islamic societies commonly are (or are tending to become).

Not quite. Even in Christian cultures female sexual display was very often stopped after marriage. Around the Mediterranean and in Eastern Europe the dress of matrons and widows was—and sometimes still is— dark, sober and colourless. A married woman was off the market, symbolically dead, and no longer any kind of topic for a novel-writer. She is simply not *interesting* any more.

I return from what may easily become a digression in order to summarize this discussion and report a change of view. For some years I have been describing 'the limits of life', in a very traditional and broadly 'platonic' vocabulary, as being temporality, contingency and finitude—or in popular language, Time, Chance and Death. I probably took the phrase from Slavoj Zizek, who says somewhere in his writing about Schelling that as after Hegel modern philosophy has tended to bring everything down into history, so philosophy's chief interest has shifted away from the old concern with timeless necessity and *a priori* truth, and towards temporality, contingency and finitude. In short: less concern with pure Reason, more concern with freedom and the 'agonistics' of the actual human condition.

I now see two objections to this. First, the continued use of the old terminology strongly suggests that modern philosophy is not yet as fully emancipated from platonism as it likes to pretend. Why must it accept from the past a blighted, devalued human life-world? At the very least, I now want to reject the notion that there is something deeply unsatisfactory and wrong about the fact that we live in time, and the fact that we are finite. I don't see how we could ever have supposed that things might conceivably have been otherwise. Of course persons are finite, and of course personal life is temporal!

The second objection is that modern philosophy has continued to be 'platonic' in another important but easily-overlooked respect: it assumes that when you are talking about human beings, the human condition, and the human life-world, what you always have in mind as standard is a free adult male in the prime of life. Heidegger and Sartre go on doing this just as much as do the writers of the old Plato-to-Kant epoch. And insofar as I have gone along with them, I too have been asking the religious question, about how we are to find the courage to live and to say Yes to life in clear recognition of life's limits, *only* from the point of view of a free adult male in the (admittedly rather late) prime of life, in good health and so on, as if the answer that will do for him will in principle do for everyone.

But we should not make that 'platonic' assumption that there is one standard and representative human type, whose deal with life can serve as a proforma for all other human beings, whatever their age, sex, condition and so on. Until recently I guess I tacitly assumed that I could write as if for anyone, but now I have four grandchildren and am highly immersed in the life of three different generations: I am in my early seventies, my children and their partners are forty-ish, and their children are in early infancy. Imaginatively, I am compelled to realize how different our situation-in-life may be for us at the many different stages of our lengthy modern lives. We cannot now say that one single religious outlook will serve, with only minor *ad hominem* or *ad feminam* adjustments, for everyone throughout life. On the contrary, the religion of ordinary life needs to be age-related. We need to keep renegotiating our deal with life, as we pass through its many and varied stages. As ordinary language says, **Be your age!** Which being interpreted means: 'Don't knock yourself out, trying to deceive the world into supposing that you are younger than you are, because that is a recipe for unhappiness. Renegotiate your deal with life, and find the way to be happy and to say Yes to life that is appropriate for you at your present age, and with the capacities that you actually have.'

That said, I now say that the classic universal limits of life, with which everyone must always come to terms, are simply contingency (or chance), and death. The kind of deal we strike with life will vary greatly according to our sex, our sexuality, our age and our condition, so that the relation to life (as I call it) needs to be almost continuously rethought as we pass through life's many stages. This continuous rethinking may seem burdensome, but it teaches us the interesting and important lesson that life as a whole is much bigger and more interesting than any one of its stages. And there is the bonus that we don't waste the second half of our lives in fighting a futile losing battle against the passage of time.

8

LETTING BE

Everyone knows that human beings are intensely sociable and imitative. A few weeks after its birth we may be struck by the way a baby stares solemnly and unblinkingly at the nearest human face. Soon it will be trying to imitate, as best it can, almost anything we do. We make use of this imitativeness in teaching the child to speak, and are rewarded by seeing with what great determination and rapidity it acquires the mother tongue and becomes a participant member of its language-group—a considerable intellectual feat.

Thereafter the imitativeness persists throughout life as we instantly and uncritically adopt all the new words and phrases, new fashions, values, technologies, beliefs and deep assumptions that come into circulation. During the past twenty years it has seemed as if the whole of society has moved together in assimilating the new communications, information, and entertainment technologies. Despite other inequalities between them, in developed societies the great mass of people are about equally schooled in an enormous body of linguistic, technical and behavioural skills. We are very highly socialized, and must be for the whole system to work as well as it does.

All this suggests that human beings have a very strong drive to 'self-socialization'. We want to learn all the rules and to join the group. We want to belong, to become integrated. But there is a snag: it is very often precisely these contexts where we should *most* like to see everyone co-operating and everything running smoothly, that bring out a savagely wayward, exhibitionistic and destructive streak in human beings. The Internet is a brilliant and very powerful invention that has spread around the world like wildfire—but it is everywhere plagued by hackers, hoaxers, viruses, fraudsters and so on. The community gives to everyone the power to call out the ambulance and fire services—and over half the calls they make are hoaxes. At home we find that 90% of the email messages we receive are junk which has to be deleted unopened.

It seems then, that we humans have a very strong desire to be accepted as members of the group. We are very willing to learn and to keep all the rules; we want to be just like the others. But we also have an equally strong desire to break the rules, and even to sabotage the institutions on whose smooth running our own well-being depends. We want to build, but we also want to destroy.

Nevertheless, because we are so sociable we do tend to assume that human beings must be happiest in their most intimate relationships. We want to idealize small face-to-face communities—the family, the village, the congregation, the residential community, the religious society, the common room, the mess, the club, the fellowship, the friendship group. Often we seek personal happiness through membership of some such ideal community.

. . . And often we are disappointed, as we discover that the society we have joined is riven by feuding factions, by power-struggles, by backbiting and bullying. Perhaps this is particularly true of academic and of religious societies, which have a strong image of themselves as conflict-free, 'cloistered', calm and supportive. It seems that Sartre is right: *L'enfer, c'est les autres*—Hell is other people, and the closer people get to each other, the more they are in danger of getting locked into attitudes of frigid, permanent mutual detestation. Religious bodies are especially Hellish in this way.

Why? It seems that in the face of life's uncertainty, death's certainty, and the instability of all valuations, we feel desperately insecure and threatened. Everyone else feels the same. To alleviate our distress and anxiety, we all try to gain some relative advantage vis-à-vis other human beings. We want *power and authority* over others, but if that is not readily available, we'll settle for *recognition* by them; and if that is not available either, we will settle for *respect*, the absolute minimum. Unfortunately, all the others seem determined to overvalue themselves and to undervalue me. So society becomes a *bellum omnium inter omnes*, a war by each against everyone else for social dominance and recognition. Everyone is bitterly resentful, everyone sees himself as a victim of injustice. We join some religious or ethnic liberation group in the hope of finding sweeter and more harmonious relations there, but unfortunately the same conflicts recur. Indeed, it is usually the case that the groups that are most idealized turn out to be the worst. In general, the lesson is that we should beware of any group whose members all claim to be 'brothers' of each other. Remember, the first murderer was a brother.

I conclude, then, that we should not look to solve our problems by joining some ostensibly perfect community that will redeem us by giving us all the love, and support, and above all 'respect' that we demand. No, the religious question needs to be tackled first, and the religious question is one that each of us must tackle alone.

The religious question is the question of life and my life. I have to learn to understand and accept the flowing, purely-contingent impermanence of everything in the life-world, including myself. I am only a mortal like everything and everyone else, and quite soon I'll be gone. But until then I have a personal stake in life, namely *my* life, which I need to claim and to appropriate as my own. By loving life and living it to the full, I can do a little to revalue my corner of the common world, and that is all I should ask. There is nothing whatever to be gained by obsessively demanding, or seeking to attain, social dominance, or recognition, or respect, and we should purge ourselves completely of such ambitions. We are nothing but our own brief performance as parts of the flowing, contingent, imperma-nent life-world. There is no substantial, enduring core-self, so there is no point in efforts to raise its standing.

Nor is there any point in pursuing the dream, popular in the nine-teenth century, of gaining salvation by slotting ourselves neatly into a close-knit, highly interdependent, 'organic' kind of society, and there finding contentment in fulfilling a predestined social role. It is too late for neo-medievalism, too late for socialism, and too late for any kind of corporate state. We are not that kind of person any longer. What we need is an open society, governed by laws and not by men, in which we can all trust the system to permit us the personal space—that is, the personal religious and expressive freedom—which each of us must claim for ourselves and grant to others. When each of us has the personal space that we need in order to be able to recognize and to solve the religious question for ourselves, then we will be able to relate to others in a solar way, loving them *without* seek-ing dominance, or recognition, or even respect. In this sense, then, religion precedes politics.

All this also applies even to the closest family relationships. In these relationships, which are so close that in many ways they are constitutive of us, it is all the more important to remember to give to other people their own needed personal space. In unsuccessful countries where life in the public realm seems permanently corrupt and stagnant, men are notori-ously prone to compensate by becoming the more whiskered, domineering and violent in their private life; but everywhere, spouses and parents are only too apt to be possessive, interfering, jealous and solicitous—without knowing it. There's a tendency to believe (in the teeth of the evidence) that domestic life is innocent and redeeming. So, once again I insist that the first thing a third millennium person must have is the personal religious and expressive freedom she needs in order to strike her own religious deal with life. This means learning to be solar, and so learning how to love without damaging or imprisoning the one you love.

First we must learn to let it be; then we must learn to let *people* be; and then we may be ready for love. We should not be looking for a tightly-knit, organic kind of society to redeem us. We should not be looking for any kind of perfect society with which to identify ourselves, and we should detest every form of ethnocentrism, nationalism, and exclusive religious allegiance. Instead, we should look for a society that is above all, cool and free, *really* free, so that people have the personal spiritual space to recognize and deal with the religious question for themselves, and to become creative. Only when that priority has been established can we begin to talk about love of the solar, non-destructive kind.

9

IMPOSSIBLE LOVE[9]

Immanuel Kant started a tradition in modern philosophy by arguing that there are certain attractive illusions to which the human mind is perennially prone. He argued that it was important to demonstrate in detail just how these illusions arise, and how they can be exposed and dissolved.

His idea here is that his *critical* philosophy is also a *therapeutic* philosophy: it sets out to cure us of illusions that very often lead people astray, and it helps us to remain within the proper limits of thought. The presumption that it is always better to be disillusioned and to see things just as they are is almost universal amongst philosophers, but in religion there is a long tradition of wanting to allow people at least some powerful guiding stories, some helpful images and supportive promises. It is not easy in religion to argue that it is always better to be an iconoclast, and to destroy illusions (or images) even in the case of the most vulnerable people. The philosophers may say that it is therapeutic to cure people of their illusions, but many religious teachers will retort that in religion weak and vulnerable people need all the comfort they can get from images and from illusory beliefs such as the belief in life after death, the belief that in the long run good will prevail, and the belief that in our moral struggles divine assistance, or Grace, is available to assist us. Even Kant himself went on to endorse qualified, ethical versions of these three beliefs, saying that it is right for us to act *as if* they ought to be and therefore might be true. As a philosopher, Kant knows that illusions are illusions, but as a moral teacher and a human being he is well aware that we all of us need encouragement.

The two greatest illusions that Kant has in mind in his main discussion are the traditional metaphysical ideas of God and the Soul: of God as the infinite spirit, the objective unifying ground of the world and self-explanatory explanation of everything, and of the soul as a finite spirit that grounds and unifies all our varied subjective experience and our changing, developing life in time. These two ideas are companion ideas: God is the infinite spirit out-there that unifies and sustains the objective world, and the soul is his finite counterpart within us that unifies and grounds our subjective life. Both are simple, both are immortal, and both transcend the two great realms of experience—objectivity and subjectivity—that they ground and unify. But for precisely that reason—that is, that they transcend experience—both ideas are empty, Kant holds. And his demolition job has proved permanent, because the main traditions of modern philosophy stem from Kant and in effect presuppose all or most of his leading doctrines. From Hegel onwards many people argued that all our life is *historical*, and that all human ideas and beliefs are subject to continual historical change. It is therefore a mistake to suppose that from our standpoint within history we can make contact with and commune with a timeless Absolute that stands right outside history. Then in the twentieth century the same argument was repeated with reference to *language*. All our mental or intellectual life is transacted in language. But the world of language is a great field of differences, everywhere shifting and changing as the human life-world and human relationships shift. In language we are always within secondariness, and can never make definite contact with anything primary and absolute.

Kant himself had believed that he had escaped from such 'relativism'. He believed that in the free moral commitment of the will we can and do make a blind contact with the Absolute which he called 'moral faith'. But Kant's ethics was the very first bit of his philosophy to be dumped by his successors, because it is so obvious that our ideas about value are *also* subject to continual and surprisingly rapid historical change.

Today it is, I think, obvious to most people that the human life-world has changed and is changing, to an extent that has destroyed all the old 'absolutes' and 'certainties' people once lived by. There are too many religions, too many gods, too many revelations, too many conflicting interpretations, all of them obviously historically-conditioned; and there is no absolute or fully-independent criterion to help us check which if any of all the candidate absolutes might be the real thing. All of which was already said by a contemporary of Kant, G. E. Lessing, in his play *Nathan the Wise* (1779), and nowadays it is commonplace. The rise of the novel and of realist drama on stage, screen, radio and video during the past two centuries bears witness to the coming of a world in which most people have become content to live immersed in the flux of life and to evolve their own personal philosophy of life as the English evolve their case-law—that is, piecemeal, out of accumulated experience. It has made the English astonishingly unintellectual, but I have to admit that it doesn't work at all badly—provided that it is conjoined with a decent presumption in favour of scepticism, which it usually is.

There remain, however, one or two areas in which we are tempted to believe ourselves in touch with something that is out-of-the-ordinary to such an extent as to be sublime, or even genuinely transcendent. The sublime is typically something in Nature of a grandeur, a storming energy, or a beauty that overmasters us, boggles the mind, makes us dizzy and fills us, perhaps, with unbounded cosmic emotions of awe and dread or pity. Something sublime in this sense is quite often encountered in everyday life, in art, in people's behaviour, or in natural phenomena; and it can affect one very deeply.

Here is an autobiographical example from about 1948. Walking on a very frosty spring morning I noticed a wren's domed nest in a hedge, and saw that it was occupied. Opening it a little, I found a wren sitting on her clutch of eggs, frozen to death. I was intensely moved, as a young boy might well be, and I remember the incident even now. But of course such a touching revelation of animal devotion even unto death is perfectly compatible with a completely secular and naturalistic outlook. And the same is true of the sublime generally.

In matters of love, however, we do seem to make, or at least to imply, transcendent claims, especially when we find ourselves remaining obdurately in love with a non-existent or impossible object, or find ourselves making impossible, transcendent claims about our love for something perfectly ordinary, such as a fellow-human being.

To take *love for an impossible object* first, a classic example of it is the continuing love of the bereaved for someone who no longer exists. One may remain incurably in love with a former partner who is dead, and even very sceptical people will agree that our own dead parents continue to be vivid and powerful presences in our imaginations. Almost equally common and vivid is our love for God, continuing even after we have realized that God never could have existed, because his metaphysical attributes and his personal attributes exclude each other.

One can still love God even after the Death of God. People do. Often they still pray to a God whom they know does not exist. Even an atheist may call towns like M in the East Midlands of England, or S in the West Midlands, 'godforsaken', because God can remind even atheists of himself by his own 'conspicuous absence' from a place. So even straight atheism cannot help but be a form of belief in God, even where it is clearly under-stood that God (logically) cannot actually exist, just as when you enter a recently-dead relative's study his very death, of which you are quite sure, makes his presence-by-absence in his study all the more poignant. Derrida calls all this 'hauntology' or 'spectral theology', and he is right.

Two other impossible objects of love may be mentioned very briefly. One is our continual love for the old religion, the faith of one's youth that one can no longer hold. As it slips away, our love for it gets stronger and stronger: Anglican peace, Catholic devotion to Mary, and (perhaps the greatest of all) the now-lost experience of Protestant joy. The second of these impossible objects is the animal with whom one may suddenly find oneself in deep accord. It is brief, it is impossible, it can come to nothing, but it is astonishing. Two entirely different worlds, two different creatures, briefly intersect in a moment of 'star-friendship', but there is no more that can be said about it. It may be an inherited capacity in my family.

Now we need briefly to explain the kind of *love that makes impossible claims for itself*. This is human sexual love, especially in marriage, which seems almost invariably to make impossible claims. When we married, we were expressly reminded that marriage is terminated by death. It is only a temporary association: it is not forever. But we seem to wish to protest against death by claiming that sexual love can be forever, as when poets promise to immortalize their mistresses, and husbands give eternity rings to their wives. In China a golden wedding celebration is a very subdued affair because everyone knows that it can't go on much longer; but in the West we are less honest, and prefer to go on pretending even after a golden wedding anniversary that the marriage will continue indefinitely.

In truth, heterosexual love seems always to want to attempt the impos-sible: like religious faith, it yearns after a *totum simul*, a pure, mutually-transparent, living presence of each to the other that goes on into eternity, an absolute love. Indeed (to take Derrida's ideas a step further than he him-self took them) in religious faith, in heterosexual love, and in all our loves quite generally, we seem to insist on making the classic, perennial mistake of Western Reason after Plato and Parmenides: we yearn for the Absolute.

There is a neat demonstration of the 'impossibility' of heterosexual love in Steven Soderbergh's film *Solaris* (2002), a fine remake of the Tar-kovsky film of 1972, which in turn was based on the novel by Stanislaus

Lem. Of these three items, the new Soderbergh film is comfortably the best—contrary to all our usual suppositions in such matters.

In the film, then, Dr Chris Kelvin is a psychologist who has been called out to help the crew of a spaceship that is doing an apparently routine job, orbiting and surveying the planet Solaris. Something is going wrong: the crew are troubled, and they hope Kelvin will understand and explain to them what is going on.

He arrives, settles in. During his first night's sleep he dreams of his wife Rheya who died by suicide just a few years ago. She was very beautiful, but she was also a troubled, withdrawn character. Her inability fully to respond to him had led to tension between them, and perhaps he partly blamed himself for her death. So he dreams about their relationship. Then someone gently wakens him, and there she is, *alive*—and seemingly not just an hallucination, but bodily, fully alive again. Shocked, he questions her, but she is evasive about details. We are together, we've always been together, she says.

Gradually, we gather what the explanation of all this is. Solaris, the entire planet, functions like a huge and very powerful brain. It has the power to pick up our dreams, our desires and our memories and to turn them into beings of flesh and blood. (Perhaps the planet is a metaphor for the mighty Hollywood dream-machine itself.) All the crew of the spaceship are in the same fix: in their cabins they each harbour a mysterious, puzzlingly-real dream lover. Kelvin is falling violently in love with his new Rheya who has come to him, and he battles to protect her when the others begin to think that perhaps they should destroy their phantasms, and flee away from this very dangerous planet.

Kelvin has a lesson to learn, and even Rheya herself helps him to learn it. She is merely the creature of his own desires, his own memories and needs. He loves her so totally only because she is *not* the real Rheya, but merely his own dream of her. The real Rheya included all the things that his love couldn't reach, all the things that led them into frustration and conflict. As for the false Rheya, she is so perfect that she explains that she is only an illusion, and he must give her up.

The point here is very neatly made. Our desire for perfect heterosexual love with a real Other, our desire for perfect mutual knowledge and love, is confused and contradictory. If you think you have found perfect love, then its object cannot be a real person, but only your own dream. Real heterosexual love has to be imperfect, just because the other is so very Other.

To put it coarsely, the otherness of the Other is indeed very sexy, and that is a great consolation. But it excludes perfection. We never achieve perfect knowledge of another person, and least of all when the other is of the *opposite* sex.

In short, all dreams of attaining perfect communion with something absolute are dead. We have to learn to love things, and people, and lives that are always secondary, imperfect, transient, and never fully understood or mastered.

Religion

10

THE SOLUTION

SOLAR LIVING

When he came to think about human evolution, Charles Darwin asked himself what might be the biological function of our moral and religious ideas. How do they help us to survive, and why are they so tenaciously held? Darwin takes his answer at least partly from Schopenhauer's essay 'On Religion', saying that a people's god is an object rather like the royal standard that is raised in battle on a long pole. On the flag is the people's most sacred symbol: it represents the supreme focus of their loyalty. It is that which unites them, their rallying point, and that for which they must live and fight and die. As long as it still flies, all is not lost.

That is a good image, no doubt suggested by the fact that the English word 'standard' can be used to describe both a flag and a norm. Its implications are realistic, in that the standard is a public object outside ourselves towards which we gravitate and to which we must remain loyal. But it might be understood non-realistically. Republics still have national flags, but whereas the royal standard belongs to and represents the Monarch, the US flag represents something less concrete, a cultural complex of institutions and ideas—the Republic, the Constitution and American values. British soldiers fight for the Queen: American soldiers fight for the American way, and indeed for the idea of America.

That point aside, we are reminded that hitherto religion has nearly always involved joining with others in attaching yourself and giving your loyalty to some great central public Object. Conceptions of the religious object are very varied, but most often it is a god who inhabits a distinct, sacred, supernatural world. And it is of course precisely these basic ideas about religion that have collapsed completely in the last few generations. There is not literally any God, or god or other spirit out there. There is not any substantial soul or core-self in here. There is no ready-made world, formed and already working. All we have is the formless flux of raw experience—think of it, perhaps, as the flickering, spotty, visual field you see if you suddenly shut your eyes tight; or call it white noise, or call it Be-ing—and out of this meaningless crackle and splutter in our afferent nerves we have somehow together managed over the past few tens of thousands of years to build our common world. We've had no external or independent help: we've done it all just by talking to each other! To get an idea of the feat this represents, just ask yourself if *you* could write the software for converting the stream of tiny electrical flickers in your nervous system into your experience of living your life in our common world. How on earth did we do it? However did we even manage to get in touch with each other?

We did it as the first signs (words, symbols) began to move—which happened the first time a flicker was read as a sign. A spark jumped across. Out of the flowing motion of language there have gradually emerged all our ideas about the world, each other, and our own selves. Our ordinary language gives us our basic world, the outsideless world of everyday life. The much more disciplined language of science, with its closely-defined vocabulary and standard method, gives us a much more elaborate continuous picture of the world—but only within certain limits, for it soon becomes apparent that the world-picture of natural science has the disadvantage of being much less friendly and human-centred than is ordinary language, but with the corresponding advantage of enabling us to act very much more effectively, and to invent very powerful technologies. So science is a very good thing, and we should stick strictly to it, but it doesn't by itself tell us how to live, nor does it by itself help us to find the courage to live and to make our brief lives worthwhile. It doesn't place us in the world, and it doesn't give us any values to live by. It doesn't get us out of nihilism.

For remember, we really *are* nihilistic now. We are in the Void, empty, derelict. There is nothing at all out there prior to us but the empty outpouring flux of prelinguistic white noise, a mere efflux of jostling possibilities, and there is the ceaseless motion of ordinary language, which gives our everchanging ideas about ourselves and our world. So in the end all we have is the stream of life, and our own lives to live within it. Culture has of course over the millennia proposed to us various rallying-points, religious, ethical and political, but we have long known that they too are all of them no more than temporary human fictions, transient like ourselves. Above us, there is only sky, and the sky itself is just the Void. That (in more senses than one) **is it.**

So what form can religion take? If there is only life, which is a movement of signs, and my own life, which is just one identifiable strand in the whole process, then the task of religion is to give us the courage and strength to commit ourselves wholeheartedly to life. Only we create the world, and only we can redeem it. By solar love of life we can inject meaning and value into life for everyone.

This means that the old religions of salvation were telling stories, not about what God had done for us, but about how *we* should live. God, you will recall, was faced by the Nihil and conquered it by becoming creative; and God gave value to the world by loving it. So that's what *you* have to do by solar living, in an age when human lives are in one sense larger and richer than ever before, but in another sense are pervasively threatened by unhappiness, meaninglessness and depression.

When they feel threatened by gloom and despair, ordinary people are apt to rely upon good company, or just upon a good night's sleep, to revive their spirits. When we are young we can usually rely upon this natural faith in life. But as we get older it begins to fail, and we need religion, not to comfort us with lies about another life elsewhere, but to give us the will and the courage to live this life to the full, and to give us the religious imagination to irradiate this our only life with religious meaning. As for other people who are despairing or depressed, the best thing we can do to help them is to lure them out by showing them an infectious passion for life.

Thus, on the view I am proposing, the sacred world of religion and the world of everyday life have now coalesced, to give us a single, seamless and outsideless whole. In the process we move on from mediated religion to immediate religion, as the whole gateway or transport system between this world and the next disappears. We can drop scriptures, creeds, doctrines, the Church, the whole cadre of religious professionals, the sacraments and public worship. That whole mighty apparatus, originally intended to mediate religious reality to the laity (from *laos*, the common people), has over the centuries come to regard *itself* as the religious object, and has become old and oppressive, sealing people into the very state of religious alienation that it was supposed to cure. In one form and another around the world, organized religion still manages to keep a large percentage of humanity locked in the most wretched mental poverty and backwardness. The best that you can say about organized religion is that its spiritual consolations help you to endure the utter misery to which it condemns you.

Solar living frees us from all that. It teaches us to accept one-way linear time, life's contingency, and death, without complaint. Instead, we should cast ourselves heedlessly into the flux of existence. We should burn, burn and burn out with love for life, a love that tries so far as possible to be everywhere affirmative, and nowhere allows itself to be turned into disappointment, resentment and hostility.

The reason for this demand for a purely-affirmative attitude to life can be briefly stated: those who split the world between good and evil in effect split their own psyches too, and the puritans, the wowsers, the morality-campaigners, the condemners and persecutors end up as unhappy people, Bible-bashers who are themselves without religion.

In this connection we should remember that until as recently as the twentieth century the Earth was not fully explored and every human group still tended to see itself as a clearing in the forest surrounded by an endless dark and fearsome realm of wild beasts and monsters. To this day there are many who say: 'We are the good people, and those people overseas who reject our values are under the domination of evil powers. By fighting them we will be defending ourselves and our way of life.' But when the exploration of the Earth was completed and the whole planet became connected up into a single communications network, everything changed. Instead of seeing Culture as a precious island of light and civilization surrounded by a vast, seemingly-endless realm of dark and threatening Nature, we began to invert everything. The human conversation that we call Culture or civilization now encloses everything, including the whole of what remains of wild Nature. Human talk has become the primary reality which today is wrapped around everything else.

That is an amazing shift. It began to happen in philosophy with figures like Wittgenstein, and we are now beginning at last to work out the difference it will make to our religious outlook.

We declared that solar living is, or tries to be, purely affirmative. It is also purely *expressive*. That is, we are not labouring to purify our souls so as to be ready for the Day of Judgment, and we do not spend our lives in forging a unified self to be a kind of monumental achievement. No, there is no Soul or Real Self, because everything that we are is flickering, shifting and ambiguous. The only way in which we can get ourselves together and become ourselves is in and by our self-expression, through which we put out, or present, images of ourselves. But as soon as I have expressed myself time moves on, and my expressed self must be abandoned without regret, because of course solar living requires us always to move on and never to become 'attached' to any version of ourselves. Solar living lives by dying all the time, as it continually leaves selfhood behind. That is how it conquers the fear of death, by making a full acceptance of death into part of the way we live. Never allow yourself more than the most transient satisfaction with a completed work before you move on and immerse yourself in the next.

11

THE SOLUTION

HUMANITARIAN ETHICS

People sometimes object that my solar ethics is too individualistic, or is not a complete ethic. That is a misunderstanding. I am using 'ethics' in a rather seventeenth-century way, as Spinoza and Traherne used it, to mean a spirituality: a way of understanding, orienting and conducting one's own life. The idea is that before going on to social relations, we need to get our individual selves sorted out first. We learn that there is, ousidelessly, only life, the world of our common human and historically-unfolding life, and within life there is my life, my part in life. So the first question in spirituality, or personal ethics, concerns my understanding of my own life and the way I am to relate myself to the greater stream of life of which I am part.

My life turns out, of course, to be subject to the general conditions of life: it unfolds in one-way linear time and is everywhere subject to contingency. A vital condition is that life is everywhere a process of *exchange*, which is essential to the constitution and the maintenance of my very fragile existence as a person. In addition, whereas the stream of life in general may go on indefinitely, my own life ends in my death.

How then should I relate myself to the general stream of life of which I am part? In the past metaphysical beliefs about God, the human soul, and the eternal world have encouraged people to think that it may be desirable and possible to drop out of life, or at least to drop out of various kinds of exchange, in order to withdraw into solitude and concentrate upon the eternal salvation of one's own soul. Nowadays, however, there is no eternal order, and the older forms of asceticism are all historically obsolete. The only remaining valid form of religious life now is by solar living: unreservedly committing oneself to the outpouring flux of life, loving life and living expressively by continual self-outing. In the process we may still try to achieve a religious and unified selfhood, but we can do so only by continually leaving our own self-expression behind us and moving on. We can in this way achieve only a retrospective self-realization: we are not to become attached to our own products, but must learn to move on and to be 'easy, going'. Thus we give up the old idea of gaining eternal life for our souls, and replace it with the new idea of getting into the habit of speaking better about this or that thing or person.

Along these lines then we can develop what I may call an ethics of active revaluation. If we listen carefully to the language, we will soon learn that a comprehensive valuation of life is already in place, and that it is confirmed in one detail or another by almost everything that anyone says. Our language teems with implicit valuations, which we urge upon each other. But many of us are not content simply to confirm received valuations: we try to introduce new idioms, and to change the ways in which some things are customarily spoken of. The upshot is that each generation somewhat shifts the overall valuation of life that it inherits; and thus gradually over the generations everything changes.

On the account just given it is very noticeable that for us values and moral realities are to be found only in language, and that they are purely human and historically-evolving. There is nothing unchanging in ethics: on the contrary, everything is being continuously renegotiated. The overall valuation of life is a matter of life-and-death importance to human beings, and since we have already argued in earlier pages that our first and greatest need is the need to feel that our own life is worth living, we can now formulate a general moral principle as follows: For the sake of our own and of the general well-being, we should do and say what we can to raise the overall common valuation of life as much as we can, and as high as is self-consistently possible. By our hobbies, our enthusiasms, our loves and our campaigning we can do something to enhance the value of our own corner of the world; and if everyone does something similar, then life as a whole is made that bit more valuable and worth living for everyone. So, as in spirituality we learnt how much we need to be able to say yes to life and to live affirmatively, so now that principle of spirituality runs straight out into a general principle of public moral behaviour. So far as you can, for everyone's sake always talk things up rather than talk them down, because on the whole the more we can talk things up and make them more precious, the happier all of us will be.

On the very simple argument just given, I have located the ethical, not out in anything purely objective, but simply in the flowing conversational exchange which is the stuff of human life. I am being careful not to suggest that anything is timeless or absolute. Nor on my account is there one standard moral Law for everyone, for on my account one can do good in one's own corner of the world in many different ways. Now we take the same argument further. Each human being learns a mother tongue and belongs to a language group. Each human being has an approximately equal stake in life and each human being therefore has a part to play in the maintenance and the revaluation of the whole life-world. There is therefore a *prima facie* case for saying that as speakers, as world-builders and as value-creators all human beings should be considered approximately equal. But of course people turn out in practice to be extremely unequal in power. Religion, tradition and various political and economic forces plunge many into a state of bondage and destitution in which they remain trapped for life. But just because each human being has an approximately equal stake in life and contribution to make to the value of life, the wretched state of many humans affects us all. It is rational to try to do something to ameliorate their lot, regardless of their gender, race, colour or whatever.

In this way again we do not ground moral obligation in anything superhuman, nor in any of the respects in which we discriminate between human beings. We ground moral obligation simply in bare, value-needing co-humanity, irrespective of gender, race, creed or moral desert. Within the general flux of life human beings are highly interwoven with each other. Emotions and valuations are highly infectious, and one person's misery darkens everyone's day.

So in a nihilistic time when all older moral theories have lost their traditional objective grounding, humanitarian ethics almost alone remains reasonably wholesome and clear. The main alternative to it is Nietzsche's aristocratic ethics of life: but Nietzsche's humanism is a Greek humanism of admiration for the strong and the beautiful, whereas my humanism is language-based and in background Christian and democratic.

A corollary is this: In seeing moral obligation as the claim made upon us by a needy fellow-human 'irrespective of gender, race, nationality, creed, or moral desert' we signal our view that popular contemporary notions of human 'identity' should be seen as morally irrelevant, and should be avoided like the plague. Humanitarian ethics likes anonymity and disclaims identity. Like a soldier on United Nations peacekeeping duty who sets aside his national insignia and wears only the blue beret, so a solar person should disregard and disclaim any self-identification with a particular national or religious or other such group. Our moral posture and practice must never be associated with a claim to be 'one of the good people', or 'a woman', or an adherent of some particular ethnic or religious group, because all those who retreat into 'identity' have given up universal morality and have embraced some form of partisan fundamentalism—which means paranoia and hatred of humanity.

I say this and put it strongly, because solar ethics is admittedly non-realist. It has no objective ground in reality or in pure rationality. Instead it is subjective and emotivist. But *for that very reason it remains determinedly universalist*, and the point is very important.

12

THE SOLUTION

ART

Parents who neglect to have their children baptized, and seem indeed to be reluctant to give them any sort of traditional religious education, sometimes excuse themselves by saying: 'We thought it would be better for him to choose for himself when he's older'. When I was a serious young cleric I used to think that attitude deplorably lazy. I felt sure that one ought to give a child a definite religious education, and that one ought to be loyal to one's own tradition. Now I think differently. Those parents weren't merely neglectful: they were broadly correct. Being baptized into a ready-made creed, adopting at second-hand religious beliefs formulated long ago by other people, is a waste of time. When you find yourself in really severe difficulties you will find that second-hand beliefs do not avail. They melt away. The only ideas, thoughts, convictions that stay with you and give you real support are ones that you first formulated for yourself, and have already tested out in your own life and in conversation with others. In effect, the only religion that can save you is one that you have made up for yourself and tested out for yourself: in short, a heresy. Heresy, heresy is the way to salvation. It alone can give us the fortitude that each one of us will need one day.

This observation prepares us for the idea that a modern religious person is compelled to be more like an artist than a soldier. A soldier joining the army fits into a pre-existing institution and learns to wear its uniform, keep its rules, share its values and obey its orders. In that spirit the Christian believer was for centuries described as *miles Christi*, a soldier of Christ. He was a realist, perceiving the whole of religion as a ready-made reality to which he adapted himself. Today, as critical thinking dissolves away ready-made 'reality' in every sphere, the believer's situation is quite different. He or she is more like a modern artist, who is confronted by nothing but a sheet of paper or a lump of raw material and must build something out of it. In a nihilistic age we don't need obedience, we need the creative imagination to build for ourselves some kind of habitation.

The point needs to be developed further. In tradition-based societies people gradually build up, and then cling fiercely to, a strong sense that their whole culture and their world—all their communal ways of seeing things and doing things—are divinely instituted, divinely-sanctioned and supremely real and immutable. What may have begun as a successful action becomes a personal habit, and then a custom that many people follow. In time it next becomes an established tradition, and then a sacred duty, and finally it is canonized as Divine Law, sacred and timelessly-valid. Along this route, the whole of Culture eventually comes to be seen as Nature, divinely established, sacred and unchanging, like Eastern Orthodox Christianity. For quite a long period this method of building up and fixing a successful culture and communal way of life can work well. And, of course, it gives to people a very strong sense of reality.

Although modern Western science is critical, and originally developed out of dissatisfaction with the world-view produced by traditional thinking, there are some similarities between the way tradition accumulates and concentrates its world-view, and the way science does. Like an Army, science is rather disciplinarian and hierarchical. Its vocabulary and its methods of working are highly standardized, and are guarded by professional academies, rather like the Vatican's 'Congregations', which define and defend standard language, method, and teaching. The result is that many scientists develop a strong sense of reality, and tend to fall into the habit of thinking that the world as it is seen under current theory is *the* world, absolutely. This is not entirely accurate, because (as the best scientists always know) theories are only human constructs, and the ones that work best just now may well not be the ones that will work best in a century or two's time, but in practice many scientists are inclined to realism. They tend to suppose that their current communal ways of describing and interpreting the world more-or-less accurately copy the way the world is absolutely. They tend to see Culture as Nature, and to that extent there is some danger that science—if it is unchecked by philosophy—may itself eventually develop into a stagnant sacred orthodoxy.

Whereas traditional, disciplinarian and communal ways of thinking always tend to turn Culture into Nature, critical thinking works in the opposite direction, constantly pointing out that things which you believed were permanent, objectively-real and sacred are in fact no more than local cultural creations, effects of the way people in your area have got into the habit of seeing things. As Karl Marx once remarked, the criticism of religion is the beginning of all criticism; and, taking Marx's ideas further, Michel Foucault neatly showed that if you can gain a clear philosophical understanding of the way the Roman Catholic Church establishes and maintains a 'régime of truth', you have learnt how to understand almost everything. You have a key to the whole history of ideas in the West, and you are of course a left-Nietzschean nihilist: 'the last truth is that there is no truth', and all our truths are merely effects of power.

In the short, dazzling period between the death of Nietzsche and the outbreak of the First World War, the nihilism of Schopenhauer and then (much more) of Nietzsche had an enormous effect upon young artists. If critical thinking dissolves away everything, if there is no Real World out there, then the artist has absolute freedom and indeed has therefore the sacred duty to recreate the world. That is why in the German Expressionist painting of the Blaue Reiter group we see so much of the classic iconography of the imaginative re-creation of this world: gaudy *fauve* colours, wild animals and birds, the circus, the jungle, the Garden of Eden, and naked human innocence.

It was a delightful springtime, brutally snuffed out by the outbreak of the War and the speedy death of some of the leading artists in the group—especially the still-lamented August Macke. But the dream of a renewal of religious innocence by the artistic imagination was at least a century old, and is met in a whole range of interesting minor figures from William Blake and Shoreham-period Samuel Palmer through to Henri Rousseau Le Douanier and Stanley Spencer of Cookham-on-Thames. Inevitably, official, organized religion did not want to hear about it, did not want to have anything to do with it, and made sure that it did not catch on. Old religion in steady decline has hitherto proved to be a fierce opponent of religious renewal, and its psychology of decline becomes more malignant with each year that passes.

Today, sadly, anyone who remains serious about religion needs to break with organized religion or, alternatively, to maintain no more than the most tenuous connection with it. Instead, we must look to art and the use of the religious imagination to enrich everyday life.

13

THE SOLUTION

COMING OUT

Solar living reverses the direction of much traditional spirituality.[10]

The Axial Age (c. 800–200 BCE) was a period when people were much impressed by the violence and potential destructiveness of the passions, and by the difficulty of achieving any stable society or lasting personal happiness in this world. The religiously-serious person sought by ascetical practices to unify the self by bringing the passions firmly under the government of reason, and withdrew from the world in order to find happiness by contemplating God or the eternal realm. In this context spirituality was typically *introvertive*. Withdrawing from the distractions of company, change, and sense-experience, you recollected yourself and waited for long periods in a state of empty alertness or 'silent regard'. Eventually you might enter a light trance, and experience feelings of warmth. To feel this warmth was to be touched by God.

Successfully practised, this kind of religious activity can be very good relaxation-therapy and very good for one's character. But whether any *cognitive* claims can be made in connection with the psychological states to which it leads remains highly questionable. The mystic very often believes that in the silence and solitude of contemplative prayer he or she has gone beyond language to achieve an ineffable, wordless, communion with the Divine. But that claim is meaningless, because there is no meaning, no truth, no reality, and no knowledge outside language. Any talk about, or even allusion to, what is outside language is already impossibly paradoxical, because the phrase 'outside language' is itself wholly *inside* language. The mystics are merely projecting their own religious 'over-beliefs' onto their own feelings of warmth: they are not gaining any fresh knowledge.

Today the traditional introvertive spirituality is widely neglected, largely because the appearance/reality distinction and the contrast between the merely-apparent visible world of human life and a supposedly more-real spiritual world within have collapsed. There is only one world, the human life-world, the world our language gives us; and this world of life is our only home. In which case spirituality must reverse its direction and become *extravertive*: that is, in order to get ourselves together we have to go out into expression. Insofar as we succeed in expressing ourselves fully and well, we may have the happiness of recognizing something of ourselves in the work that we have just produced. If we are aware that our self-knowledge is very imperfect, and that we are very often a prey to sharply-conflicting feelings and impulses, we may rejoice to see in our product a more unified and generally much-improved image of ourselves. Thus we learn that the effort of producing the work has been personally therapeutic. But as I have been insisting, we cannot cling to this briefly gratifying self-image. Time moves on, and so must we. Solar spirituality is therefore a life-long work of self-expression that must continually move on, and may never cling to the occasional compensations and moments of joy that it encounters.

Solar living, on this account, is completely worldly. It is ceaseless, self-expressive, world-building activity. It is like art or writing, which are never finished. One simply goes on doing one's thing for love's sake, and *for life*, in more than one sense. You never get there: there is no reward. But then, the painter, the novelist and the rest of them all know that the work to which they are dedicated is endless. Nobody will ever paint the last painting, and nobody will ever write the last poem. Nor will there ever be a definitive public valuation of the worth of one's own work. There is no cosmic Final Examination. Solar living is, as the phrase goes, 'its own reward', and we shouldn't think of either asking for or expecting any absolute Recognition. All human beings seem to crave some kind of public and objective recognition and commemoration of themselves and of the worth of what they have done. Often they think of their names as being written down in a cosmic book. But if we pause to think about it, we will see at once that the way life is makes it quite impossible that we should ever get the kind of external confirmation or ratification that we long for. Language is always a living and changing thing, and it does not permit us the kind of stable, objective reality and order of values that we would like to have. Being solar means fully taking into your soul that final victory of relativity and nothingness—and *then* saying an all-out Yes to life, and living as creatively as you can for as long as life remains. Our life's work must be like an artist's in being productive symbolic expression, and in being done just for the joy of it and without any external endorsement at all.

This discussion has also committed us to giving up the traditional distinction, going back at least as far as Aristotle, between a person's outer social life with others in the human world, and her 'inner', 'interior', 'spiritual' life, a secret history of the soul that is known only to God. For all sorts of reasons we need to insist that I am just my own life with others, which is a life of continual symbolic exchange. Language (and linguistic meaning, and truth, etc.) is all public, and I just *am* the role, or the *persona*, that I play in our common life. I am my outside: what you see is all there is, and I don't have any 'mind' or second interior life that is of any consequence. All that needs to be said of the 'mind' is that it is what is there when we 'bite our tongues' and withhold the words we were about to utter. Thinking is a running-in-one's-head of possible but incompletely-executed utterances: thinking is a rough draft, and often no more than what writers sometimes call a 'splurge' draft, an uninhibited rush of gut-opinions that we must prune down severely in order to fix upon what we will actually choose to say. Speaking for myself, I'm afraid that my 'thinking' is nothing like as good as my writing—and when we realize this we see that the whole platonic idea of the intrinsic superiority of a supposed interior world of pure 'thought' is (and always was) tosh.

So you are what you say, you are your own self-presentation, and your religious life is identical with your outer life of public utterance. By creative solar living we can hope, to some extent, to get ourselves together—but only in a way that we must continually leave behind as we move on. In the past, I have called this retrospective redemption, or 'post-sainthood', meaning that actual, achieved sainthood is an impossible dream, and that we can never achieve more than the partially-unified selfhood that we can sometimes briefly glimpse in our work as we produce it and then promptly leave it behind.

Does this sound too severe and pessimistic? I am insisting that our living is always in motion, and never comes to a final Everlasting Rest; always a work in progress that never reaches perfection; and always in secondariness and relativity without ever coming to its Last End. I insist upon that, but I also insist that if we fully accept the limits of life and then learn solar living despite all the bad news, then we truly will occasionally experience eternal joy in the midst of transience. In this again we are like artists, whom we envy, not because they enjoyed earthly recognition and success, but because their commitment to their work made their lives utterly enviable in spite of **everything that life threw at them.**

14

ETHICS WITHOUT ANY
OBJECTIVE VALUE

Our moral values, important though they are to us, have no foundation in Nature, nor in any metaphysical order that is independent of human culture and human language.[11] The main reason for saying this is that orthodox scientific method is 'the only game in town': i.e., scientific method (and, behind it, critical thinking in general) is far and away the best and most powerful way to knowledge that human beings have so far come up with. Setting aside for the moment the question of the precise status of its 'findings', so far as knowledge is concerned science is unrivalled; and from its point of view there is no objective purposiveness built into the world and no cosmic moral law. Nor is there any objective and fully-independent foundation for, or endorsement of, our valuations. In short, so far as our best contemporary knowledge is concerned morality and moral values belong entirely to culture and not to nature, and morality is a human institution like the civil law. It is cultural, historically evolved, and still evolving very rapidly.

During the 1960s, if not earlier, people in general became aware of the extent to which moral valuations are already built into the language and the idioms that we inherit, and therewith of the extent to which by a determined effort we can *change* received valuations. For example, in 1960 it was still possible for a group of boys playing some boyish game to exclude someone who was trying to join in by saying to her: 'No, you can't. You're only a girl.' In 1960 it was still possible to say something like that innocently; but not today. Our appreciation of that phrase, 'only a girl' has changed utterly, and a great deal else has changed with it.

A whole new approach to ethics thus comes into view, and I can summarize it as follows.

No society is quite without morality. There is always a general social consensus about the desirability or otherwise of a very large range of things, qualities, behaviours and character traits, a consensus that is clearly audible in the ways people speak. It is what people call the social or public sanction, because it puts pressure upon us all to behave and to judge things in generally-approved ways.

The whole set of valuations of everything at any one time may be called that age's 'overall valuation of life'. It often includes obvious and even severe inconsistencies, and we may have all sorts of reasons for feeling discontented with the current valuation of something. If so, we can argue or campaign for a change in the way that thing is customarily spoken of and treated. Such arguments may very often resemble arguments to the effect that the civil law ought to be changed on a certain point, or that a particular painter or poet is currently underestimated. But three vital points need to be noted about all such arguments, whether they are about morality, or about reform of the law, or about literary and artistic values. First, all three institutions are merely human and historically-evolved. Secondly, we don't have to suppose that in any of these areas we are dealing with things 'absolute' and 'timeless' that somehow transcend the flux of human conversation. On the contrary, morality is just talk, the law is just talk, and art is just talk: in all three areas opinion is permanently in flux, and truth is just the current consensus. But thirdly, it does not follow either that argument is irrational or that our opinions are 'merely' transient fictions. On the contrary, art, morality and the law obviously matter a great deal to us all, and it is equally obvious that sometimes arguments for major change in our customary valuations can be very strong and can thoroughly deserve to prevail. For example, in the past few generations we have seen strong new arguments producing major social change in values in such areas as feminism and environmentalism—and this, despite the fact that the arguments either way could rarely, if ever, make any significant appeal to 'foundations' either in Nature, or in metaphysics, or in pure reason.

Thus in morality, in aesthetics, and in law you don't need to be a realist, you don't need to be a foundationalist, and you don't need to be any sort of Platonist in order to care about your topic and make a real difference to it. On the contrary, you are much more likely to be able to bring about significant moral change if you believe that morality is changeable, rather than if you are a cranky conservative who thinks that his own mindless prejudices are eternal verities, and demands that everyone else must immediately submit to them. The cranky conservatives always assume that they stand on the moral high ground, and in truth they have historically often occupied it; but their record in occupation is deplorable, and it's a thoroughly good thing that we historicists and relativists managed to tip them out.

On this point, I venture to disagree with no less a person than Derrida (and some others of his generation). He was inclined to think that reason itself is systematically biassed in favour of 'logocentrism', 'ontotheology' and realism generally, both in metaphysics and in ethics, so that the antirealist and the 'deconstructivitist' are always at a disadvantage and can never achieve a clean and complete victory. Perhaps for this reason, Derrida in his later years lapsed a little on the question of justice. But I think he was wrong. I think we postmodernists, relativists and nihilists must keep our nerve, and go for victory. Otherwise, the West will lose its way, and badly. I mean, *really* badly.

Now to return to the main argument. It *is* possible rationally to argue for a change in the currently-prevailing public valuation of anything, and it is possible to win the argument. Generalizing, we now lay down the rule that a solar person who loves life should argue for and live by as high an overall valuation of everything and everyone around her as is consistently possible. That is, we should completely eliminate from religion its historic concern with detecting and combating sin, uncleanness, evil and the rest. Instead we should try so far as we can always to be affirmative and magnanimous, and never to be resentful, or grudging, or unforgiving, or even disapproving.

The two main reasons for this policy are obvious. When we try for as high an overall valuation of life as possible, we are trying to be sure that we hand over as good and happy a world as possible to the next generation. That is the single best thing we can do for them. And the second reason for trying to be as consistently affirmative as possible is that the record of religion in the past in sniffing out and denouncing sin, and persecuting sinners of every sort, is so disgracefully bad. No religion deserves to survive unless it has entirely purged itself of that mentality. The 'negative emotions' poison the soul of anyone who indulges them.

I am of course not denying that some crimes are so threatening to society that they must be detected and punished. What they are, and how they are to be dealt with, should be left to the normal processes and institutions of a liberal democratic society. Its sanctions should be sufficient, and my present argument has merely been to the effect that we don't need a whole lot of superadded religious sanctions on top of the civil ones.

Why the Old Religions Are Now Dead

15

RELIGIOUS BELIEF-SYSTEMS AND POLITICAL IDEOLOGIES

In 1771 Richard Arkwright established at Cromford, Derbyshire, England the first successful mass-production factory, a cotton-spinning mill worked by water power. Thereafter technical improvements came rapidly, as the mills began to weave cloth, as factory buildings began to be built around strong and fireproof iron frames, and as canals and then, later, railway lines were built to bring in raw materials and carry away the finished goods. But from the very outset competitors were grasping the enormous economic potential of Arkwright's factories. Only two years after the first of them began production, a curious German came to inspect it, and a replica was built and actually in production in Germany before the 1770s were ended. Arkwright attempted to protect his ideas by using Patent Law and various security measures, but it was in vain. The first industrial revolution soon became an unstoppable social and economic force.

The second industrial revolution may perhaps be seen as beginning with the 'space race' between the USA and the Soviet Union in the 1960s. It is marked by the accelerated development of computers, and the establishment of a ring of large and powerful communications satellites around the Earth. Very rapid, very cheap, and very high-capacity means of data storage and retrieval, and of communication, quickly became available to almost everyone, all around the world. From the 1990s people everywhere were seizing upon the new technologies with great enthusiasm. They seem to be bringing about the development of a single world economy, a single world conversation of humanity, and the dominance everywhere of the English language. The web is also a powerful democratizing influence, because it gives to so many people a cheap and easy way of starting a business, or of publicizing their own ideas.

The first industrial revolution spread rapidly, and soon had very great social and political effects; but the second revolution seems to be spreading even faster, with cultural consequences that we do not as yet see clearly. The first industrial revolution is usually seen as having had a powerful secularizing effect, especially upon the new industrial working-class that it created, and one might expect the secularizing effects of the second to be even greater, as extreme cultural globalization overwhelms and dissolves away all merely local ethnic and religious traditions. Surely the new technologies are already creating just the new world view and philosophy of life that this book describes?

Maybe. Perhaps we are indeed going to see very rapid 'detraditionalization' and globalization all around the world, and especially among the young; but it is evidently not happening without any resistance. Already one version or another of 'identity-politics' is appearing in many parts of the world, as communities battle to affirm and preserve their distinct ethnic, cultural, religious or linguistic 'identity' against the threat of dissolution by assimilation. And, as we see already, when traditional religious belief is called upon to be at the heart of a people's struggle to preserve their historic 'identity', it begins to take on the role of a political ideology.

Now when traditional religious belief is conscripted into the service of some local cultural tradition with which it has long been associated, and is viewed as a kind of political ideology, then religious faith becomes a matter of obligatory political loyalty to 'your own' people. Debate about whether your religious beliefs actually merit rational assent, and apologetic arguments generally, are out of place. Nobody wants to hear such talk. Religion as supposedly constitutive of your people's historic identity must be clung to in its most hard-edged form, non-rationally and with total loyalty. That is fundamentalism, religion turned into something like extreme nationalism and clung to, not because it is seriously thought to be true, but because it is politically necessary. On marginal points, a 'party line' is laid down. Sadly, over the past two or three centuries, as every major religious tradition has experienced a sharp decline in its intellectual standing and credibility, fundamentalism has come more and more to look like the only likely future for any of the old religions. After all, no top-level rational apologetics is being written today, or ever again will be written, for any of the great old religions. Nor can they inspire any great new art. What other future can there possibly be for them *except* as 'heritage' or as fundamentalism? Already amongst Jews, Christians, Muslims and Hindus it is the case that respectable, seriously-religious and relatively rational practice is being outshone and outvoiced by the noisy extremists, who have so far perverted the values of the old religion that there is even a case for saying that they are not really *religious* people at all. Don't we already live in a time so secular that the old creeds are not intelligible to most people *unless* they are read as ideologies of political struggle for political survival and independence? Alarming though they are, the 'extremists' seem to most people to make more sense than the genuinely-traditional 'moderates', whose religion sounds merely well-meaning and weak.

It is hard to avoid the conclusion that in the short run the extremists or fundamentalists will prevail. By appropriating what remains of the old religions to their own purposes, the fundamentalists will in effect finally destroy them. But when they have done that, the fundamentalists will also destroy themselves, because the stolen clothing they wear will no longer be gaining them any credit or credibility. In the long run, then, all localist reactions against globalization will fade, and the religious outlook and philosophy of life that we are describing in this book may be expected to prevail generally. Indeed, it is already doing so.

In this chain of argument two points need to be pursued further. First, why does its conversion into a political ideology do an old religion so much damage? The problem is that in the modern national state the politician's overriding duty is to strengthen the state and to secure its survival, its independence and its long-term prosperity. The state, it seems, has to be a thoroughgoing rational egoist, whereas for a religious person there are always things that matter more than one's own life. A religious person may dedicate her life to a cause, or give it on behalf of another, whereas it is surely unthinkable that any politician should ever commit *the state* to a course of self-sacrifice.

Thus in a recent conflict apologists for the state of Israel argued, as they have so often argued before, that Israel can lose only once. In every war the very survival of the state of Israel is at stake—which means that Israel is morally justified in resorting to whatever means are necessary in order to win the war. The bombing of civilian areas of Lebanon, a country with which, as such, Israel was not even formally at war, and the killing of large numbers of entirely innocent women and children, was therefore justified. But suppose that the same moral question be put to an *individual,*

Jewish or not: 'Is saving your own skin so important to you that you would consider yourself justified in slaughtering large numbers of women and children in order to achieve it?'—then the absurdity is obvious. At the *individual* level, nobody could contemplate such a preposterous suggestion. It therefore seems beyond doubt that when religion, battling for its own survival, allows itself to be translated into a messianic political ideology its own best traditional values must promptly be eclipsed by the nation state's appalling egoistic imperative.

The second question to be asked is about just how far back the use of religion as a political ideology can be traced. It is certainly arguable that religious institutions have had many important political functions ever since the rise of the first city-states six thousand years ago. In an often rather untidy way, religion validates political authority, shapes time and space, functions as a focus of social loyalty and a tool of social control, and so on. Religion tells you who your god is, who your true king is, who and what you must obey and fight for, and what your values are. In fact, religion is the original seedbed of almost every aspect of 'ideal culture': it may not invent and prescribe all your technologies or all your leisure activities, but it does, or once did, almost everything else.

True enough. But we live in a time of comprehensive cultural globalization, when religion is chiefly being used for reactionary localist purposes. It keeps battling to return us to old 'identities', old forms of oppression and old enmities. As such, the old religions increasingly look like threats to future human well-being.[12] In this book I am simply attempting to describe an emergent non-political and fully-globalized form of religion that will fit us for life in general and for social life, *without* sectarian rivalry and conflict. Maybe you think that the religion of unmediated commitment to life is no more than a para-religion. But the old religions have already died, and the unpleasant politicized fundamentalisms that have replaced them cannot be endured for much longer. Eventually, the religion of life will be the only faith left.

16

THE CIRCLE OF LIGHT,
THE SURROUNDING DARKNESS

Imagine a brightly-lit walled city surrounded at night by many miles of darkness, or, going further back in time, imagine a large bonfire in a forest clearing, with a crowd of people huddled in a circle about it. They sing and talk, looking only at each other because they are relying upon the central fire to push back and keep at bay whatever may be prowling around in the surrounding dark. If they are suddenly attacked they will very quickly seize a brand from the fire, and with it turn to face and repel the enemy.

In this ancient and powerful image the central fire and focus of attention is the god, and the whole lit-up circle that he creates is culture, or 'the City'. The fearsome encircling darkness is the wild, or wild Nature. The picture implies that the tamed, domesticated, familiarized, human-friendly realm is an enclave that religion has established for us. First the god took up his position and established his own Holy House, and then from that point he fought back chaos and old Night, establishing an ordered, well-lit and safe realm for us to inhabit. Our city develops around his house. He is the author and the true king, but as the years go by he prefers to live more quietly and delegates the day-to-day work of kingship, first to a college of priests (this form of government is technically called hierarchy, from *hiereus*, a priest), then to a demigod, and ultimately to a merely-human being. Thereafter, Temple and Palace, Altar and Throne, stand side by side about the central square in the heart of the City. Light and order radiate outwards from them.

It is still implied, however, that the encircling Darkness, 'Chaos and old Night' remains. It is bigger than culture, and even older than culture. And it is very noticeable that the people in the Centre are convinced that they alone are in the light, and all the rest of the world is dark, chaotic, and generally under the rule of the Devil. We alone understand, the light *we* live by is the only true light, and there is no good life for humans except the life that it lived by our law.

This conviction that clear vision and moral virtue are to be found *only* among one's own people, who are by definition one's own co-religionists, remains extraordinarily strong to this day—especially amongst Evangelical

Christians and amongst Muslims. Many Muslims, especially in the Muslim heartlands, really *do* see what they call 'the West' as a place of profound chaos and darkness. Only they are in the light: we Westerners are lost souls, groping blindly. It is an outlook that will only begin to break down as, over the millennia, people gradually become aware of the effective reality of other religions, other clearings in the darkness, and other gods.

Perhaps one can become aware of the reality of other religions only by the development of critical thinking, and the possibility of setting one foot outside one's own tradition in order to see how the world looks to someone else.

Alternatively, the image of the lit-up clearing in the dark forest suggests the possibility that perhaps as the generations go by and different clearings grow larger and larger, they may eventually join up, until at last the human-ized cultural realm gets to be bigger than the wild. England, like Holland, is a country whose entire landscape is all man-made and cultural. There are no fully wild areas left—and indeed, there haven't been for some centuries. During the twentieth century, it became possible to think that there is now hardly anywhere left on Earth that remains completely wild.

And now, much more important, by the late twentieth century a person with a decent scientific education and some knowledge of social and economic history can begin to understand that we have now learnt to understand and to read in terms of human theory everything in sight, both in town and in the country. The whole world has become Culture, lit up by human theory, covered over with human language, and appropriated to human beings. Culture is everywhere, and it now encloses Nature in such a way that we begin to see that we humans are the true creators. Our descriptions and our theories have made all the world ordered, intelligible and brightly-lit. Instead of being frightened of the old wild forest, we now battle to conserve the surviving bits of it. We are now responsible for look-ing after it, for we are now aware that *we* are more of a threat to *it* than it is to us.

In this new situation one can see how awkward it is that so many people are still trying to posit and to live by versions of the old, exclusive One-God-one-Truth-one-Sacred-Law picture of the human condition. It is hardly surprising that Muslims, Evangelicals and the more conservative Roman Catholics all agree in being permanently at odds with the modern Western culture that is all around them, but is just outside the circle of their own thinking. They all see people who are not of their own 'obedience' as being in darkness, moral laxity and spiritual confusion. So they are always prickly, always hating the cultural world around them. They want to regard it as dark and full of monsters, even while they are all the time drawing numerous benefits from it. Even the most violently anti-Western Muslim still uses Western electricity every day, and could not manage without it.

So, in order to get out of that unhappy relationship to one's own time one must get out of the old kind of religion, and into the new and far superior religion of life.

17

WE THE GOOD PEOPLE;
THEY, THE OTHERS, THE EVIL ONES

People love to take sides, and symbolic battles between good and evil, between the good guys and the bad buys, are and will remain popular in religious mythology, in genre entertainment, in epic literature written for children, and in political rhetoric.

Where does all this material come from? Three main stories can be and are told. *The history-of-religions story* usually begins with the dualistic mythology of the Persian prophet Zarathushtra (c. 500 B.C.E.). There are very great and well-known scholarly problems with the available sources for Zarathushtra and his teaching, but we are usually told that the prophet maintained that, as well as the good eternal spirit Ahura Mazda, there is also a co-ordinate and also-uncreated evil spirit, Angra Mainya. The two are locked in perennial conflict, which continues in the present age of human history, and before very long will rise to a climax in the Last Battle, which will be won by the good people. They will live for ever thereafter on a renewed and perfected Earth. These ideas deeply influenced first Jewish, and then in due course Christian, apocalyptic thinking especially in the Latin West. The two most influential works of Latin theology, Augustine of Hippo's *The City of God* (c. 400 C.E.) and John Calvin's *Institutes of the Christian Religion* (1536 C.E., and later editions), both expound Christian doctrine as a mighty Grand Narrative history of salvation, telling the whole Story of Everything as a prolonged struggle between that which is at God's Right hand, and what he sets at his Left hand. Election and Reprobation, the City of God and the City of Man, eternal salvation and eternal damnation. To this day American Protestantism shows its Calvinist background in the way we hear Republican Presidents address their fellow-citizens as 'the good people' who are pitted against 'an evil empire' of foreign persons overseas. The politician can safely assume and his audience will always know that 'the majority of decent hardworking American families' just *are* 'the good people', and that their opponents out there must be evil. The President's language picks out a large body of voters, consolidates them, and uses an echo of apocalyptic language to build up their moral confidence that under his leadership they are divinely destined to prevail over their opponents. He is invoking a story twenty-five centuries old, but it still works; and for as long as it continues to work politicians will continue to use it.

The second story about the origins of dualistic thinking suggests that human thinking everywhere builds up and structures its world in terms of *binary contrasts*. Almost any word can be and very often is made clearer by regular citation of its autonym, as when we speak of up and down, left and right, male and female, light and darkness, sameness and difference, positive and negative, and so on. It is indeed striking that so many words come in contrasting pairs in this way. Surprisingly often we hear people saying things that imply that everything really *needs* its Other, and must have its Other. Thus in religious debate we sometimes hear people defend the belief in evil spirits by arguing: 'If there is a force for good at work in human life, surely there must also be a force for evil?' Conversely, Evangelicals will seize gratefully upon any evidence of (or at least of people's *belief* in) the working of *evil* supernatural beings and forces, because they see it as helping to make more plausible their own faith in a *good* supernatural order. It was for this reason that some twenty years ago certain Evangelically-minded professionals helped to give currency to the belief in 'child satanic abuse'—with very unhappy consequences. To them it had seemed that a cultural climate in which Satan was widely agreed to be at work was a climate in which people might the more easily be persuaded that the Grace of God was *also* at work.

Binary thinking of the sort we are describing seems to wish to build up the Other—the counterpart, the opposite number—as a mirror image, or an inverted replica. In the early Middle Ages, when Islam first threatened France, Christians had only the vaguest notions of what Muslims believed. So they presumed that if Muslims were their enemies, then Muslims must worship their own diabolical Trinity, 'Mahound, Termagant and Apollyon'. Bizarre, but even today almost equally absurd fantasies can be entertained in relation to a religion of which people know little. Thus the Western Press is well-disposed towards the current Dalai Lama, but knows little or nothing of Buddhism. So it often assumes that his religion must be Catholicism's oriental Other, and speaks of him as a 'god-king', a mixture of Christ and the Pope.

In religion, at least, binary thinking can evidently lead us into some very odd mistakes. But it remains surprisingly popular in modern physics, where there remains a marked tendency to try to arrange the fundamental particles and other postulates in binary opposed pairs.

The third historic stand in dualistic thinking is *ethical*, and is well illustrated by the still-popular phrase about 'teaching children the difference between right and wrong'. The idea here is that every normal, healthy human being needs to be morally aware and morally *active*: that is, one does not just indulgently accept everything in life for what it is; no, one must actively discern and discriminate, sift and separate good things from evil things, always choosing and cleaving to the good, and rejecting all that is evil. Everything needs to be sorted into one or the other of the two great camps. A truly moral person, one of 'the good people', is a person who is *actively moralistic*, everywhere and all the time dispensing approval or disapproval, praise or blame, love or hatred. That is what God is like: he is a judge, a critic (from Greek *krisis*, judgment). He separates: he knows where to draw the line. We are not to be taken in by all the chatter about 'shades of grey': no, the world must be seen strictly in terms of good and evil, and it is one's moral duty to be morally officious.

A disposition of this kind is nowadays often called 'puritan', and (perhaps correctly) people associate it especially with ultra-conservative Islam and with the various strands in Protestant Christianity that have been influenced by Calvinism. In theology, it is perhaps grounded in the awkward confrontation between a Creator who is pure and unmixed perfection, and a created world that is very complicated, mixed and often blighted. Surely God himself must be actively at work to overcome evil and to restore and perfect his world, and if so, then surely the people of God have a duty to be actively and officiously moralistic, sniffing out and denouncing threats to public morality, and fearlessly criticizing other people's sins?

On this point, there is a very ancient dispute in Christianity between those who believe in a folk church that is a school for sinners and which is tolerant of human weakness and human diversity, and those who see the church as a society of saints, fully-converted and righteous folk. Roughly speaking, Catholics, Anglicans and Lutherans take the former view, whereas the thoroughgoing Protestants who descend either from Calvin or from the various groups of 'Brethren' take the latter. The present-day controversy between 'moderate' Islam which is friendly to culture and the applied arts on the one hand, and 'extremist', Taliban-style Islam on the other, seems to be very similar. But notice that for all parties in both traditions God himself will in the end decisively and finally separate the good from the evil. And of course both traditions confront the initial paradox: how can an infinitely-holy God bear the sight of a world made by himself that has become so mixed, and now contains so much that is evil?

In short, if you are a strongly realistic ethical theist, you are obliged to be a 'puritan'. You must urgently desire to make the world fit to be inspected by its Maker. You will be a small-town dignitary, cleaning all the carpets and curtains and repainting everything in preparation for a Royal visit.

But from the point of view of the religion of life everything looks very different. We want to leave binary thinking and the puritan mentality behind us as completely as possible. We want to be as purely and universally affirmative as we can. We want philadelphia without xenophobia, as magnanimous and uninhibitedly-generous as possible. The long-established faith-traditions that people call 'the world religions' are in truth scarcely 'world' at all, for they are all rooted in merely local histories, local languages, local ethnicities, and local customs, and virtually all of them divide the world between 'we', the good people, the faithful, the umma, the people of God, and they, the heathen, the kaffirs, the goyim, the godless, unclean, and benighted outsiders. And it is precisely that kind of thinking that we must leave behind us.

So I envisage that the new fully-globalized religion of life will have no institutional embodiment at all. It does not need a power-elite of trained religious professionals. It does not wish to divide the world, either between insiders and outsiders, or between the holy and the common. The only base that it requires is simply the daily conversation of globalized humanity. In that arena, people will come to it spontaneously.

18

GOD OF LOVE, GOD OF HATE

If God is perfect, infinitely pure and holy, then anything that is other than God, or differs from him in any way at all, must be less perfect than he is; indeed, it must be *infinitely* less perfect than he. It must be utterly repugnant to him. How can pure, infinite, selfsame holiness tolerate difference and otherness?

Suddenly we realize that a God who is infinitely holy and perfect must also be infinitely touchy. He must intensely dislike anything that is alien to or different from himself, and he must be driven instantly into a state of furious wrath by any direct and open criticism or opposition at all, *just as his followers are.* In recent years we in the West have found that the elderly religious leaders within our minority ethnic communities are extremely sensitive to any kind of open criticism of their faith and customs, and are demanding strong blasphemy laws to protect their own feelings. As God is infinitely touchy so also, nowadays, are the people of God. When, suddenly, deep offence is taken, God and his people alike flare up in a sudden explosion of outrage. Buildings are burnt down and blood is spilt.

Only a paper-thin partition separates talk of a God who is infinite love and compassion from a God who is pure implacable hatred—a thought which suggests that we should refine one of the central doctrines of the dynamic depth-psychologists. They—figures like Freud and Jung—used to point out that the emotions or instinctual drives tend to come in binary pairs: tenderness and violence, love and hatred, appetite and nauseous disgust, life-wish and death-wish. When one of a pair is pressed too hard or becomes too strong, *or is sharply rebuffed,* it may suddenly tip over into the other. In such a case we are liable to speak of 'the rebound', and to quote the stock example of a woman obsessively in love who when jilted suddenly becomes an avenging Fury. My general point is this: the classic doctrine states that the basic emotional drives come in binary pairs so related that when one of a pair is pressed too hard, or is blocked or frustrated, it may suddenly tip over into its opposite. And the complementary doctrine I add is that the more intensely pure and refined the feeling or quality, the more acute the ambivalence. Thus in the Hebrew Bible, in the New Testament, and in the Holy Quran the more insistently the writers praise God's infinite love, mercy and compassion, the closer we are to outbursts of violent rhetoric against the enemies of God. The more God becomes a God of pure love, the more he *also* becomes a God of pure hate. Just look at the *writing*.

Nietzsche commented on this point especially in relation to the Johannine writings, but it needs to be developed a little further. All the great Axial Age religions became large-scale systems of religious mediation. The religious life became very highly regulated, and God tended to disappear behind a mighty code of sacred Law. Theologians and religious writers often turned into jurists—as in Islam and in Orthodox Judaism they still are. But the believer who equates piety with living under rule, like a ten-year-old child who has become obsessed with keeping strictly to the rules, is apt to be very 'rigid' and intolerant of laxity. And when religious individuals or groups have become very legalistic, scrupulous and 'puritanical' the danger of acute irritability and ambivalence becomes all the greater, and a decent, conscientious search for personal integrity and purity of heart only too easily turns into an insane witch-hunt. It has happened often in the past, and it is still happening today. Purist, over-spiritualized conceptions of divine love, holiness and perfection tend to encourage human beings to become ferociously irritable, violent, and cruel.

This explains why in the present essay I have entirely abandoned the traditional dualistic thinking which opposes divine holiness and human sinfulness, and which constructs religious doctrine as the story of a prolonged cosmic war between powers of good and evil. Instead, the religion I describe accepts life as it is, as a package deal, finite and imperfect. We should avoid the zealous pursuit of ideals of absolute purity, holiness and perfection. The thirst for the Absolute is slightly mad, and in the end destructive. Instead we should always prefer things human, actual, imperfect, transient and (above all) bitterbittersweet. In ethics, I'm arguing for a practice that is as consistently affirmative as it knows how, and attempts never to allow entry to the negative emotions that poison the soul: resentment, envy, covetousness, grievance and grudge, bitterness and hatred, and all the rest. The true victory over evil is simply the practice of magnanimity. As for the bitterbittersweetness of life, try just to live with it and smile over it. Ruefully, maybe. But there are possibilities of joy in this affliction of which we are all aware.

19

ORGANIZED RELIGION

TRUTH, POLITICS, POWER

What we have been taught to describe as the great 'world religions' are ancient, regionally-based, cultural traditions.[13] What survives of them today may be more or less well-organized under a generally-recognized leadership. The most highly organized bodies are all Christian: they include the Roman Catholic Church, the various ancient national churches of Eastern Christianity, the major Protestant churches, and numerous other bodies. The Jewish and Muslim faith-traditions are also relatively well-organized, whereas in Asia the national religious traditions of India and China (for example) are very loose-knit—so loose-knit that in their case we cannot easily identify *any* recognized central organization, or leadership, or spokespersons, or body of 'orthodox doctrine' at all.

Against this background it is easy to see that whenever a (normally) 'Western' person uses the phrase 'organized religion' we must assume that what is chiefly in mind is the Roman Catholic church and the various other Christian bodies that in some degree resemble it. This dominant model of organized religion has a number of features that may have only partial counterparts, or even no parallels at all, in other traditions. They include sacred scriptures that are held to convey a special divine Revelation of religious truth, and a class of professional scribes and interpreters of scripture; a system of rituals, performed by a professional priesthood, through which each individual is established in membership of the religious community, and sustained in it throughout life; and thirdly, out of the two professional groups just mentioned—the 'clerks' who copy, interpret and preach scripture, and the priests who administer the sacraments and manage worship—there is developed a mighty system of religious leadership and 'regime of truth' by which religious truth is formulated, published and enforced, which controls worship and the sacraments, and which codifies and enforces a large body of religious law. In the fully-developed system the Church becomes a ghostly counterpart of the State; or, in the Islamic version, the religious community and civil society come eventually to coincide. Thus 'organized religion' becomes a mighty system for the overall control of human life and thought. In 'Christendom' it manages almost everything but secular sovereignty and war—in effect, it manages almost the whole of culture. Cult and culture coincide. In Islam, the religious system deals also with sovereignty and war, leaving an even smaller secular sphere.

At its biggest, organized religion in the West was indeed very big. It owed much, no doubt, to ancient secular Roman methods of organization and government. The Emperor Constantine, Christian kings in the Latin Middle Ages, Protestant 'godly princes', Russian Tsars and British Hanoverian monarchs were all conscious of using the church and its creed to validate their own rule and to stabilize the social order generally. At any rate, religious truth, at least in Christianity and in Islam, has almost always had a political character. The religious leadership have seen themselves as being the divinely-commissioned stewards of a body of divinely revealed Truth, their role being to guard it, define it, propagate it, and enforce it. They do this with such success that the people internalize the notion of a regime of truth, and come to regard any religious dissent, nonconformity or heresy as seriously threatening to the well-being of society as a whole.

All this means that, at least in Christendom, Islam and Jewry, and even (though perhaps to a much lesser extent) in the Indian and Chinese culture-areas too, religious truth has always been political. Truth is defined and enforced for political reasons, in political ways, and with certain political interests in mind. Although in the long medieval period many or even most philosophers were content to remain conforming members of the religious community, the more typical situation has been that the churchman and the philosopher are profoundly different animals who tackle questions in religious thought in entirely different ways. To put it briefly, any philosopher who is serious about religion should avoid all contact with 'organized religion'. He needs to put as much distance as possible between himself and its ideas about truth. Which is why, on the day this book is published, I shall finally and sadly terminate my own lifelong connection with organized religion.

I mention this unimportant personal matter because it has some wider echoes. During the twentieth century we learnt from the Communist Party many lessons about political ideologies, and about what it was like for Europeans to live under a vigorously-enforced regime of truth. Happily—at least, for us in the West—it has all now collapsed, and we are unlikely to see it return. But in retrospect, it has all thrown a very unflattering light backwards upon our own traditional *religious* regimes of truth, especially in Christian and Islamic societies. I think this is one reason why we are currently witnessing an accelerated 'decline of religion' in the West, and perhaps also in other parts of the world. We can no longer assume that religion in general is a good thing. Too much of religion now looks actively harmful. We don't want there to be *any* compulsory established ideology, religious or not. Increasingly, people are seeing all organized, traditional forms of religion as morally ugly, reactionary and violent, and they want to be rid of them. In the USA people are wondering why the Republican Party has allowed itself to be infiltrated, and public policy to be so much influenced, by Evangelical Christians who are (to speak plainly) thoroughly bad people. And, one may add, why in England have the Bishops been so feeble as to permit a near-complete takeover by Evangelicals of the country's oldest and best institution, its national Church. Why couldn't they put up a fight?

Already public opinion thoroughly dislikes 'organized religion', and with good reason. Which is why it does not figure at all in our outline Religion of Life. We don't want ever again to see either religious ideology or religious institutions become socially and politically established in the traditional way.

20

POSTMODERNITY

GLOBALIZATION VERSUS RELIGIOUS 'EXTREMISM'

In the 1960s, it is often said, theologians of a revisionist or radical inclination generally accepted the Secularization Thesis. The steady progress of Enlightenment, together with huge advances in science and technology, and the general ethical coming-of-age of mankind, were everywhere liberating human beings from the shackles of tradition. To survive, the Christian gospel must be demythologized and re-expressed in terms of the new world-view of secular humanism (or, perhaps, Hegel, or Marx, or William Blake, or Nietzsche . . .). The process of secularization was effectively unstoppable: resistance was useless. So said a line of writers, from Bonhoeffer and Bultmann back in the 1940s to Altizer, Harvey Cox and Robinson in the 1960s.

Half-a-century later it is widely believed amongst theologians that the 1960s marked the last hurrah of modernism. Since then, its utopian belief in the coming general liberation of humanity within history has been demolished by our new awareness of multiple dire threats to the human future, and by violent localist reactions against globalization in all parts of the world. Religion is back, one might say, *with a vengeance* and now sharply challenges the hegemony of secular reason. Marxism looks weak and passé, and resurgent Islam has come to present a greater challenge to the future of Europe than ever communism could muster. Spain, Italy and some other countries feel nervous about the future. For one thing, communism and fascism died quickly, but Islam seems to be indestructible: religion is far more tenacious than any political ideology. How can we stem its advance, except by a matching revival of our own religious tradition? So the currently-fashionable young neo-conservative theologians maintain that traditional Western secular and philosophical reason has led to nihilism, from which we can be delivered only by a ringing reaffirmation of theological reason and classical Latin Christian theology.

In summary, the 1960s radical theologians were modernists, who accepted the Secularization Thesis, and were (broadly) followers of the

Lutherans Bonhoeffer and Bultmann. By contrast, the new theologians of Radical Orthodoxy describe themselves as postmodern, and their logic owes much to the Calvinist Karl Barth.

Although the Secularization Thesis is nowadays widely regarded as a bit of liberal, progressivist ideology that has been falsified by events, there are still a few who accept it. They include the veteran New Zealander Lloyd Geering, the last Sixties radical still publishing, and the present writer. We say that new technology is if anything still accelerating the globalization and secularization of culture, and the statistical decline of the old religious institutions. As for the alleged great resurgence of religion, it is all spin and bluff. Next time you hear a spokesman invoking those 'billion' or 'one-point-three billion Muslims', check out the actual number that turned up for the last *hajj* at Mecca. Multiply it by about forty, and you have a rough index of the number of publicly active and committed practising Muslim males. Similarly, in supposedly Christian countries check the percentage year by year of infants who are baptized, or the number of marriages that are solemnized each year by the churches. In relation to the Roman Catholic church, check the average age of secular priests, or the numbers of monks and nuns. In a multi-cultural Asian trading city such as Singapore, check out what has been happening to the many places of worship over the last few decades. All the evidence is that the Sixties diagnosis was broadly correct, and secularization marches on unchecked—especially, perhaps, in Europe and East Asia. The emptiness of the great Irish seminaries is a fact even more glaring and undeniable than the recession of the glaciers. As for the much-vaunted 'return' of religion, it is a return of religion as a badge of local 'identity', used as part of a localist rearguard action led by the elderly against globalization. It is not a return of religion as *religion*. Nowhere in the world is fundamentalist or 'extremist' religion producing world-quality writing, music, architecture or philosophy such as the great faiths produced in their medieval heyday. On the contrary, it produces only tired pastiche, junk.

In short, the Secularization Thesis still stands. But I must allow that the young postmodernists of Radical Orthodoxy are correct in their claim that the development of secular Western reason since Descartes (or, maybe, from much further back) has led us to nihilism and to a time of religious crisis. The confident secular humanists still like to pretend that God and the whole supernatural order was no more than an illusion which can be dispelled without anything else changing very much. This is a bad mistake, because it fails to understand the extent to which God has underpinned a whole raft of deep assumptions around which Western thought has been constructed ever since Plato and Parmenides. The work of pointing out these assumptions and showing their new groundlessness has been done especially by Nietzsche and Derrida, and their writing has made clear to us that the Death of God is *also* the death of a readymade, objective intelligible Cosmos that we were created able to understand, the death of the true Self, of objective cosmic Reason, of objective value, of real meanings fixed out there, of Truth out there and so on.

So the young Turks of Radical Theology are right about nihilism: but they are too impatient to be able to stay with Derrida, connect him up with others like him such as Gianni Vattimo and Nagarjuna, and ask what the religious possibilities of an outlook such as this might be. Instead they go straight for a rather fundamentalist reaffirmation of what they quite uncritically and unphilosophically consider to be the revealed essence of Christianity. In this they clearly go astray, because Biblical criticism has shown beyond reasonable doubt that the doctrine of the Incarnation (for example) is just mistaken. As an interpretation of Jesus it is wildly implausible: no New Testament writer teaches it in full, and only one—St John—comes even close to it; so how do we know that it is *revealed*, as part of Christianity's permanent essence?

The rest of the classical Latin Christian system of doctrine is open to similar objections. It is all long exploded. So we are thrust back upon the problem of nihilism and how we are able to react to it. Here I argue that we should look to Wittgenstein, to Buddhism, to ordinary language and the present moment. A few months' study in late 1998 convinced me of the remarkable extent to which the consensus of ordinary people in their everyday speech has already faced up to the problem, and has evolved an informal philosophy of life in response to it. I have gradually come to understand it a little more clearly, and I am presenting it in this book. It is highly amusing to think of trying to explain it all to Friedrich Nietzsche himself, the posturing Great Philosopher heroically voyaging through strange seas of thought alone. He was indeed a grade-one genius—one must certainly allow him that—but how could one explain to him that ordinary non-philosophical laypeople in their daily exchanges have somehow succeeded in getting a little further than *he* got? The herd have outstripped the Great Man, and the tortoise has outrun Achilles. Oh dear!

21

THE SECULAR FIGHTBACK AGAINST 'BLACK' DICTATORSHIP

Under the type of religious organization that is now at last passing away, the construction of various ascending scales of holiness and spiritual power has always required the relative downgrading of the rest of the world. The value that is concentrated *here* has had to be withdrawn from somewhere else. For example, it was for more than a millennium claimed that monks, nuns and the secular clergy were somehow holier and closer to God than the rest of us, and their celibacy was supposed to give them extra moral authority. Chastity was a holy state and virginity was religiously better than marriage. But this implied a relative devalorization or downgrading of sex, of women, of domestic and family life, and of the whole secular sphere of life generally. Eventually people were sure to rebel, and indeed, of all the human liberation movements that have arisen one after another in modern times, the secular fightback to restore a proper value to everything that our religion has historically devalued is arguably the most important. It is indeed of great *religious* importance, and one may reasonably point out that a dramatic religious revaluation of the secular will in the long run be seen as Christianity's greatest achievement. It has been slowly building and gathering momentum since the Middle Ages, and in the last generation we have seen it triumph in the last solidly Roman Catholic countries in Europe. Suddenly, within a decade, the Church's power has collapsed in countries like Ireland and Spain—and it is weird for someone of my generation to find that the great cathedrals of Spain, the country's grandest architectural monuments to the Church's historic power, wealth and cultural importance, are now scarcely on the tourist map. People look away: they no longer want to admire that kind of thing or pay it any attention at all. They want to forget it.

I confess that I have felt the same myself in St Peter's, Rome. A totally irreligious building: a showy, coarse display of spiritual power. A papal theatre. I don't like the implicit values: they are detestable. And still more, I don't like the way in which other people and other areas of the lifeworld were leached of value in order to create all this. People prate about 'religious freedom', but in practice that nearly always means the absence of any proper checks on the Church's ceaseless struggle for the increase of its own power—and especially, its power over its own members. The Church's greed for power is *infinite*. Given free rein it will become more and more of a bloodsucker, without limit.

The violence of the sudden reversal of values can astonish one. Thousands of dedicated souls laboured for their whole lives to increase the size, the power and the wealth of the Church, believing themselves to be labouring Ad Majorem Dei Gloriam. For many, many Catholics the two causes have been by definition identical. But then the dreadful scandals of the Eighties and Nineties came along, and something suddenly snapped. The Irish people, for example, could no longer tolerate the Church's intense self-interest and its attitude in particular to women; and Ireland—Ireland, of all countries—was suddenly lost.

In Poland the Church was also deeply identified, in the East European manner, with the people's long struggle for survival. It was a rock during the years of Communist Party rule. But then the Communist Party collapsed. Would the Polish now see how much the Catholic Church loves human freedom? No: instead they saw it wanting its full share of control over the new post-communist society. But, said someone, 'We didn't spend all these years struggling against red dictatorship, merely in order to replace it with a black dictatorship'.

Since the Protestant Reformation was at least in part a rebellion against the Church's power and its exactions, it was at first experienced as a liberating force. But it was not long before people began to complain that 'New Presbyter is but old Priest writ large', in Milton's words. Reformed religion prated about freedom and talked about 'the Crown rights of the Redeemer in his Church', but the petty local tyranny of the Elders soon turned out to be if anything crueller and more searching than the tyranny of the old religion. Americans will think here of the writings of Nathaniel Hawthorne, and indeed it is particularly painful that so many of those who fled to America in search of religious freedom should have ended by creating, and then suffering under, new systems of religious oppression.

Against this background we can see how significant it is that the new religiosity of 'life' follows in the tradition of the Society of Friends, the Quakers, in trying hard to avoid creating either any system of government or any structures of rising grades of sacred holiness, value and power. We don't want the sacred/secular distinction at all. We don't want any religious ranking. We want an ethic that is as consistently and generally affirmative as possible. In short, the religion of life represents the overthrow of a religious order that has lasted for millennia. We want *all* life to be holy, and we don't want there to be *any* privileged persons, or places, or things. Have you noticed that today even the Pope himself can be, and is, vociferously and successfully challenged? Even he is answerable to the media.

If I stress the great religious importance of the long struggle to reclaim and revalue the secular world, you may perhaps think chiefly of the Protestant Reformation. But no, in Italy it all began long before the Reformation. Until the later Romanesque period, almost all art was sacred art. It depicts denizens of the sacred world against a gold background. They are ageless figures with bland symmetrical features, staring expressionlessly at you, head-on and without any individuality. Then gradually, over three centuries or so, the human world is recovered, bit-by-bit. Human emotion, human suffering. Then, the blue sky of the human life-world. Then interlocking human gazes, above all in Giotto. The space and time of this world: perspective. Landscape. The process of human ageing, and fully-individualized human faces. The female nude—and so far we are only up to Jan Van Eyck. Then painting slowly moves on to genre scenes, and scenes of everyday domestic life—but the last step is the hardest of all to take, and I'm not sure at what point we can be completely confident that we have at last found a totally non-ideological celebration of just plain ordinary secular everydayness. But only when that point is reached[14] have we at last seen the final dissolution of the special sacred world, and the finally-achieved redemption of *this* world. When that joyous moment comes God dies, and the history of religion reaches its End. The world, this world, *our* world becomes paradise regained.

22

SPECTRAL THEOLOGY

THE LINGERING GHOSTS OF GOD, OBJECTIVE REALITY, ABSOLUTE KNOWLEDGE, PURE LOVE, AND ETERNAL HAPPINESS

The full coequal deity of Jesus Christ—'very God of very God, of one substance with the Father . . . '—was finally agreed at various Ecumenical Councils of the early Christian Church during the fourth and fifth centuries. Since the doctrine goes considerably beyond anything the New Testament says, and also because it seems to present various philosophical difficulties, it has often threatened to cause trouble for the Church. With reason, for once the Incarnation of God in Christ had been clearly stated and officially propounded, ecclesiastical Christianity had only a finite lifespan ahead of it. The end of dogmatic metaphysics, the Death of God and the transition to a purely this-worldly religion of ordinary life had become inevitable. Thus the proclamation of the full Deity of Christ was both the highest achievement of the old supernaturalist world-view with its 'mediated' type of religion, and its death sentence.

Why? Because the new dogma asserted that God, without qualification, had made a human life his own. The Absolute, at this one point at least, had finally come down into history. Which meant that in the long run everything, but *everything*, would by Hegel and his successors be brought down into this world of time and change. The plenary Incarnation of God in Christ would by the twentieth century come to mean a complete and irrevocable switch of religious attention from God to Man, from Yonder to Here and Now, from eternity to history—and, in short, the full secularization of Christianity into a form of radical humanism, the religion of life. Christianity brings God down to earth, for good. For good.

It is ironical that the very dogma that was supposed to be Christianity's central and highest affirmation should turn out eventually to be a Trojan Horse that it had unwittingly parked in the middle of the holy City. But for some centuries the Eastern or Byzantine version of Christianity was dominant, and it tried to insist upon an interpretation of the Incarnation that would resist the slow secularization of religious thought. In the Person of Christ, it said, the eternal order has manifested itself to human beings living in time. The Incarnation was not to be read as 'the conversion of the godhead into flesh', but rather as a uniquely concentrated and intense Epiphany of God in time, in and through which 'the manhood would be taken into God'. So the Incarnation during the first Millennium was generally seen as the gateway through which humans would be lifted up into Heaven, rather than as the gateway through which the entire supernatural world would be brought down into history.

How then did the secularizing, humanistic interpretation of the Incarnation first get moving and then gradually come to prevail in the West? The art tradition indicates that the Western mind was less philosophical than the Eastern, and that we in the West always preferred to think in terms of narrative. For the Westerner, we are saved not just by the *Person*, but by the work, that is by the lived *life* of Christ. Thus to the Orthodox Christian the image of Christ crucified was an image or icon of Christ's priestly work and his victory upon the cross. The figure is often fully-clad, straight and *regnant*; whereas in the West the same subject comes to be treated as a *narrative* of human suffering that stirs human emotions, and the Christ-figure is twisted with pain. Just to look at a crucifix is to have human thoughts and feelings about a fellow-human being—and to equate these thoughts and feelings with thoughts and feelings about *God*. *Good Friday*: the most secular day in the year!

Continuing the same theme, the Eastern Christian imagination is invariably fixed upon the eternal world and the eternal world alone, as the iconostasis in an Orthodox church clearly shows. The Gospel events are static set pieces, set against a gold background without any attempt at naturalism or realism. By contrast, the Western religious imagination pictures the life of Christ as a truly human life, a *social* life lived amongst others under a blue sky and against a particular landscape background. As we saw earlier, it is Giotto above all for whom the great events of the Gospel narrative are not just straight epiphanies of eternal Truth, but human dramas with the participants engaged in eyeball-to-eyeball confrontation as they ask each other: 'What do *you* think? What do you make of this fellow?'. This isn't just divine illumination of the mind; it is finding oneself to be caught up in a human debate.

In the art of Giotto we see the beginnings of Christian humanism and of what used to be called the *devotio moderna*. The human life of Jesus was the gateway through which, during the second Christian millennium, the whole of Christianity was gradually brought down into human history and slowly turned into the new religion of ordinary life. The process took almost a thousand years, and was very complex, but now it is just about complete. We are just getting there.

Taking stock, we understand that the new nineteenth-century discovery—'everything is historical', 'all Be-ing is temporal', 'everything is immanent', 'life has no outside'—this great discovery puts an end to every form of the idea that the process of things in time is somehow controlled or regulated from a fixed point outside time. No: everything is immanent within the process; everything heaves and surges together like the sea, and a whole set of traditional religious absolutes are now lost. Because we live wholly within the temporal process and cannot jump clear of it, we have no access to any extra-temporal standpoint from which objective judgments might be made about the process as a whole, and about whether things as a whole are getting better—or, indeed, going *anywhere*.

We are always in the midst of things, and therefore the old absolutes are lost: the eternal, perfect and omniscient God; *the* world as a Cosmos predesigned for us to inhabit and to understand; a final blessedness-giving state of absolute knowledge at the end of our journey, in which we shall participate at last in the final Truth about everything; the possibility of pure love as a state of total mutual transparency and security in self-surrender to the other; and eternal happiness. Somehow, from Plato and Parmenides onwards, these 'absolutes' provides the fixed pegs between which great tropes of narrative were suspended like hammocks—which shows the justice of Nietzsche's observation that standard Western Christian theology was just 'platonism for the masses'. But now we have had the wit to ask ourselves: 'Hey, wait! How are the pegs fixed: what makes us so sure of them?' And the pegs, the fixed points, are suddenly gone. The new religion of life is the result, as everything is brought down just into the way we relate ourselves to life, now. That is all there is. Every moment is contingent, every moment is final, every moment is a moment in which we must make a decision of faith that both seizes *and lets go of* life at once. We pour ourselves out, we pass away, we experience *in passing* a fleeting joy in life. That, as they say vulgarly, is your lot. It is all there is, and it is all you'll ever know.

It is strange that I have had to add to this a reluctant appendix about our impossible loves and about 'spectral theology'.[15] But it is true: even Nietzsche himself, the great prophet of the Death of God, had to concede that the ghost of God lingers on. Religious ideas—at least, the most important ones—have a certain indestructibility about them. Ideologies get defeated, discredited and purged, and scientific theories are exploded and forgotten; but Europeans still remember the gods of the old religion even after two millennia, and in our bedtime story-reading to children we recall ideas about animals and spirit-powers that are much, much older even than that.

In the case of the old fixed points or 'absolutes' that used to govern and support Christian thought, the fact seems to be that even as we say that these old ideas are now dead, discredited and lost, we are inevitably harking back to them and so perpetuating them. Suppose I go Buddhist and say that in our world everything is utterly Impermanent, then just my saying so will still have the effect of awakening and activating in you and in me the old yearning for Something fixed and eternal. It's dead, it's impossible, it cannot exist, you can't have it, it is no thing—but still the old lost love refuses to die.

So I still love the dead, impossible God, just as I still yearn after all my other impossible loves. The problem is that because there is so much less Reality about now than there used to be, there isn't any very great difference, so far as my *heart* is concerned, between what is contingently actual, and all the crowds of other things that are contingently non-actual, or even impossible (but still hopelessly loved). Life as Limbo, where one is surrounded by importunate shades. But don't let them drag you down. **Let** (as the beautiful phrase has it) **go.** Be easy, going. To die happy: that's all there is for me to look forward to, and it is all there is for you too.

23

FORGET, FORGET!

Nowadays one quite often hears of Jewish fathers who simply do not wish to have their sons circumcised, and even of people like the American Secretary of State in the 1990s, Madeleine Albright, who in middle life learn for the first time that they are in fact Jewish—but their parents had decided not to tell them so. It is true that all around the world there are many people who feel displaced, and want to 'rediscover their roots' by returning into their ancestral culture, religion and language-group; but it is also true that there are many people who no longer see any point in carrying on their backs the burden of too much history and too much worrying all the time about whether one's own minority group is being unfairly treated. The old language, customs and all those cherished communal grievances—the old culture generally—can get to seem shabby and fusty. We might be better off just forgetting all of it. Thus in the USA there are millions of well-established people with ordinary-sounding Anglo-Saxon names who in fact have rather exotic ethnic pasts. For a generation or two in their families there was an effort to keep up the old ethnic cultures and connexions. But as time has gone by it has been found convenient to anglicize the family names and quietly forget the past. And perhaps they are right: why spend your whole life feeling victimized, quite unnecessarily?

We often get the feeling nowadays that the various traditions with which in the past we have identified ourselves were never really all that good. A visit to Venice, for example, can prompt one to see in that city an image of the whole European tradition in its present final decline. Just how good was it, and how nostalgic should we be about it? Spectacularly good art, of course—but art that sprang from a very muddled, eclectic tradition, and it was art produced chiefly for the display of wealth and power. Today many people will declare that they are not very interested in learning all about classical mythology, or even Christian mythology, in order to understand the art of a culture that is fast receding from us. And as for the social order of Venice—its politics, its morality, its policing, its prisons, its epidemic diseases—we may well wonder today why Wordsworth's famous sonnet praises the city so highly. It stinks, in more ways than one. The art is beautiful—but, but, but, there are so many buts.

Ranging more widely, in the British nineteenth-century tradition people who had just invented the history of art took great pleasure in historical architecture that enthusiastically recycled all the major styles of the past. But eventually there was a revolt against historical architecture on the part of other people who wanted to forget the past, and instead explore what new things could be done today in a new world with new materials and technologies. So we stopped putting up buildings like Barry's Houses of Parliament, and began instead to put up buildings more like Norman Foster's Swiss Re tower at St Mary Axe.

Can you imagine a similar revolt against 'historical' styles in religion and morality? Nietzsche, unexpectedly, was far too complimentary about Latin Christian theology and ethics, and indeed about the whole tradition of Christian spiritualities in the West. He attributed to it much more intellectual and moral coherence than it ever in fact had. After two centuries of modern critical theology we should have gathered the strength by now to admit that the Christian tradition is an untidy jumble, a running argument between widely-different theologies and moralities, and an 'orthodoxy' that was always incomplete, badly-made, and at key points demonstrably wrong. We should have the courage now to say. 'Forget it! Let's see if we can do better.' We used to venerate our own tradition and to consider ourselves bound by it. But now we realize that we have become very different people who live under very different conditions. Our world-view and our values have changed radically, and it is not surprising that the old religious traditions are so quickly slipping away everywhere. Maybe they did produce good art, once: but we don't want them back. What is left of them should now be relinquished for the tourism industry to exploit as it wishes. Those of us who are still serious about religion should break with the past and set about trying to create something better. And I don't want any longer to feel that gut-wrenching, guilty longing for the security and the approval of a religious institution that I know very well is only human, all too human. The old religions are not beautiful any more: they have become ugly, and people need to be rid of them. That is why I nowadays spend so much of my time with the first religious society that *doesn't* seek to lay burdens upon people, or to make them feel guilty.

Solar Living and Cultural Renewal

24

LEARNING TO LIVE WITHOUT 'IDENTITY'

In our tradition we have for many centuries tended to alternate between two styles of thinking that I shall call *globalism* and *localism*. The globalist outlook wants to see a single set of universal laws of reason, laws of nature, and moral principles prevailing throughout the whole world. But in reaction against it, localist thinking emphasises local differences, and tells us to identify with our own cultural tradition—our own distinctive vision of the world, our faith and customs. Above all, we should seek out and cling to everything that *differentiates* us from the rest of humanity, and binds us together. *Difference* is more important and valuable than *sameness*.

The contrast I am describing is familiar in the Hebrew Bible. The globalist or universalist strain, found in some of the Latter Prophets and the Writings, presents a religious vision that reaches out to the whole of humanity, whereas the localist strain concentrates exclusively upon the election by God of the people of Israel, their special task and destiny. At its most globalist, the Hebrew Bible speaks of Adam, and is a book for all humanity. At its most localist the Hebrew Bible is extremely enthnocentric, laying down all the ritual observances by which the Jews enact their difference from all other peoples, and saying to them that your own people's special relation to your God is the fundamental fact about you which must rule your whole life. For you, Jewishness comes first in every way, and humanity in general comes second. That is classical 'identity politics'.

In the more recent Western tradition, the great triumph of Isaac Newton's physics made globalism prevail across the Western world for over a century. Newton had proved that a universal mathematical physics was possible. He had shown that all local motion everywhere in the Universe is governed by a small set of simple and clear mathematical rules. Nature was an elegant and predictable machine, the same everywhere, and it seemed that the whole scheme of things within which we human beings live was well-designed and good. There were universal laws of Reason and of Nature, and it seemed obvious that our human codes of law and morals should follow the same pattern and be the same everywhere. People began to speak about international law, and to draw up declarations of universal 'Rights of Man'.

Globalism peaked, one might say, in the language of the American and French Revolutions, and in the work of the Jewish scholar Moses Mendelssohn (1729–1788), in whose day some leading Jews even contemplated giving up their separate Jewish identity and becoming completely assimilated into liberal Protestant Christianity. That is something we could hardly imagine today, for of course during the nineteenth century there was a sharp localist reaction in the rise of messianic nationalism, not only amongst the Jews themselves, but in many countries. Your nation had its own distinctive language, history, culture and art-tradition, and you must be prepared to sacrifice your life for the sake of its honour, its independence and its sovereignty. In fact, nationalism and the cult of the national spirit became an immensely powerful secular religion. Ethnocentrism was a sacred duty.

Extreme nationalism divides the whole world up into competing nations, each of which thinks only of its own interest. In time, it provokes a reaction, as internationally-minded people try to check national egoism and develop international laws, conventions and institutions. And that is roughly where we are today.

This political history has been reflected in the history of religions. The scholars of the Enlightenment were the first to construct a list of major world religions, each with its own great territory, its language, its culture, its history, its doctrines and rituals. Thus, as the modern nation-state was being invented, so the modern conception of a religion as a kind of spiritual nation was also being invented. People found themselves committed by birth to sacred territories: to Christendom, or Islam, or Hindustan, or the Buddhist world, or to what was usually called 'fetishism' or 'animism'. Language, culture, religion, homeland—these things were all part of your birthright. In the curious modern use of the term, because you identified yourself through them, you learned to speak of them as your 'identity'.

This was a fateful development, because in due course it made people around the world aware of their own distinctive religion as their own *heritage*. One had a duty to know about it, and take a pride in it, so that as in politics the concept of 'my nation' was the seedbed of militant nationalism, so people began to get militant and assertive about their own distinctive religious heritage. It's not something you question or criticize: it is something you fight for. So Judaism begat 'Sionism', Islam begat 'Islamism', Hindooism (as they called it then) begat militant BJP-Hindu nationalism, and even Buddhist monks took to the streets. It was the West that had invented the concept of a religion as a great cultural bloc that was your heritage, and through which you *identified* yourself, and it was the West that invented the transformation of objectified religion into aggressively militant ethno-nationalist ideology. So the early-twentieth-century world of warring nation-states gave way in due course to the late-twentieth-century world of warring religious 'identities', often fighting for sovereignty over territory.

It's worse than that. As during the twentieth century there was an enormous expansion of world population from one-and-a-half to six billion, technological advances, political upheavals and cheap mass travel all combined to encourage very large-scale population movements. These movements are transforming every large country—and especially every large Western country—from a nation into an empire. A nation is a more-or-less ethnically and religiously homogeneous group of people, who feel they are all of one blood, and are indeed all interconnected by descent. By contrast, an empire embraces under a single political authority many peoples of very diverse ethnic, cultural, religious and linguistic backgrounds. Thus the British used to be, and to feel they were, a nation; but now they feel the country becoming more like an empire. More than that, we realize that our modern conception of what a religion *is* commits the people of each major faith to try to build around themselves the entire social and cultural world of their own tradition. And it is indeed entirely natural that, just as Christians have long wanted to Christianize the whole of British social and cultural life, so today Muslims should want to make Britain into an Islamic country. Even the Jews, small though their numbers now are, can seek planning permission to make a whole district into an extended Jewish home by running overhead wires around it to create an 'eruv'.

A practical contradiction thus arises. Britain has become like an empire, and I for one rather like living in an empire, with all its cultural richness and variety. It's as if, nowadays, 'everything is everywhere': almost all the peoples, all the cultures and religions of the world are represented today in modern London, a city of 200 languages, just as all the varied voices and activities of humankind can quickly be accessed in one's own study. But it is not going to be possible for any one religious group to dominate completely, and to remake the whole human world in its own image. All of us now have to learn to live as members of one minority group amongst others. All of us now have to acknowledge others, and must also acknowledge the (limited) sovereignty of the state to which we owe allegiance.

When in the past many competing religious and ethnic groups had to coexist within one empire, the standard method of reducing friction was segregation. The capital city was divided into 'Quarters', and different ethnic groups lived in different villages—an arrangement that survives in many places today. But in dynamic, rapidly-developing societies segregation soon leads to inequality, and inequality leads to sharp political unrest; and my own belief is that our modern experience is showing us that we need to change our understanding of religion. We need to give up the idea that in our own tradition we already have, readymade, a complete civilization in miniature, founded on an exclusive and final revelation of Truth, and demanding our absolute and exclusive allegiance. Still more do we need to give up the idea that our very identity as persons is given us by and through our commitment to such an idea of religion. And that is what I mean by 'learning to live without identity'. We need to become *inwardly* globalized. Nowadays, when 'everything is everywhere', I'd rather lose my identity and be everyone and anyone. People who live very international lives are already learning what it is to live without identity, and finding that it soon becomes second nature to them.

Ten years ago I was asked to write a contribution to a symposium of essays on the dialogue between Judaism and Christianity. In response to that challenge, I wrote a deliberately-subversive piece saying that I was unhappy with the whole idea of there being two big things, one called *Judaism* and the other called *Christianity*, and each being a kind of finished block that is not going to change. Sorry, but no: that whole way of dividing up the religious world and talking about religious differences is now inappropriate. In our society we no longer live in one or another of a whole series of walled-off ghettoes. Everything is everywhere, and everything now mingles. None of us can claim privileged access to his own tradition: on the contrary, all your tradition is just as accessible to me as mine is to you. The whole idea of *any* privileged access to Truth is dead.

Everything is in the melting-pot, everything mingles, and I'd like to ask what will emerge from this mingling. Where is it taking us, and what kind of future will there be for religion?

Here is what I wrote just ten years ago, and what I still think today.

Is it now too late to be talking about Jewish-Christian dialogue? As it is usually understood, the phrase implies cautious, friendly conversations or negotiations between teams of somewhat elderly parties, mostly male, who represent two independent communities of faith. The aim is to find some common ground and to establish amicable relations—in short, to agree to differ, because it is tacitly taken for granted that the two communities propose to remain permanently distinct. We are coming together in order to agree upon how we can most peaceably stay apart. On neither side is there expected to be any compromise whatever, because it is taken for granted that religious allegiance is like allegiance to one's own nation, but even more so. It is both what people call an 'identity', and what people call an 'absolute'. That seems to mean that through it uniquely we identify ourselves, finding our place in the world and our task in life; and that therefore its moral claim upon us overrides all other claims. Accordingly, negotiations between representatives of different religious groups are rather like diplomatic negotiations between the representatives of distinct sovereign nation-states. The talks may lead to the establishment of peaceful, friendly and co-operative relations between two sovereign parties. But sovereignty itself remains axiomatically non-negotiable. It is an absolute, a unique 'identity', almost an eternal essence, something that one cannot envisage ever being superseded or becoming obsolete. Its claims are a matter of life and death. For their sake one must be ready to accept martyrdom, or even (nowadays) to get involved with terrorism.

This ancient idea of unconditional allegiance to some local group is still found in many forms in the late-modern world. It may be called fundamentalism, tribalism, communalism, ethnonationalism, and so on; and it creates a rather untidy picture of the human scene. The local god, or nation, or other object of unconditional allegiance to which people rally may be almost any threatened language, or ethnic group, or 'race', or religious group, or nation state; and the domains of these varied rival foci of 'absolute' allegiance may very easily overlap, and so create acute and painful conflicts in the minds of individuals.

Now I have a number of arguments to put forward in connection with this situation. Their cumulative effect is, I shall suggest, that we should give up the received quasi-political and highly reifying ways of thinking about 'the Synagogue' and 'the Church', and the dialogue between them. The very notion of 'a religion' as a small, distinct, unchanging, self-identical, closed ideological world, like an isolated sovereign nation, within which people are unanimous in matters of belief, is dead. Notoriously, we can't even say very clearly exactly who 'the Jews' are nowadays, or who might count as their officially-accredited and generally-recognized representatives. There are too many shades of lapsed membership and partial belief. And much the same is true of 'Christianity' and 'the Church'. I shall argue that the real situation is that if we want to go on thinking of 'Judaism' and 'Christianity' as distinct traditions, each with its own literature, its own body of beliefs, its characteristic style, then we should recognize that they are nowadays fast becoming entities like 'Platonism'; for as their embodiment in a distinct community of shared belief becomes ever less clear-cut, they are becoming assimilated. They are turning into relatively enduring and identifiable strands within a wider and historically-evolving global cultural tradition. As such, they are no longer strictly tied to just one territory or organisation: they are becoming public property, freely accessible to everyone, and part of everyone's thinking. In this sense I am myself as Jewish as many Jews, and as much a Buddhist as many Buddhists. Nowadays, surely, we all of us 'contain multitudes'.

A great tradition eventually comes to belong to all humankind. When, not long ago, the site of Aristotle's Lyceum was found in Athens, local politicians declared grandiloquently that the remains 'bear witness to the continuity of Hellenic civilization', with the implication that they see themselves and their electorate as the true and legitimate heirs and successors of Pericles and Plato. But in practice people around the world seem to feel able to study Plato and Aristotle for themselves, without needing to seek instruction from modern Greek politicians and philosophers. And similarly it has become very noticeable in recent years that the best writing about Christianity no longer comes from Christians, nor even from traditional academic theologians. It comes from post-Christians, and has done so for many years, because modern Christians have come down in the world since the days of their own great tradition, just as modern Greeks and Egyptians are not quite the equals of their ancient predecessors. In which case we should perhaps think of giving up the idea that 'Christians', 'Muslims' and 'Jews' are three very distinct communities rather like nation-states, each with privileged access to its own unchanging core-tradition of religious and moral wisdom. Until about the sixteenth century something like that was indeed the case: if you wanted to learn about another major tradition, then you had to travel and to sit at the feet of a learned person from within that tradition. But nowadays abundant printed books, the free worldwide dissemination of information, and the globalization of culture have made everything freely available to everyone. We can now be anything and everything. Most of us, at least, are not confined, and do not wish to be confined, to a cultural or religious sub-world or ghetto. Judaism and Christianity, like Platonism and Buddhism, are becoming strands in everyone's thinking. The old idea of an exclusive and unchanging historically-transmitted religious 'identity'—a unique body of truth in the sole custody of a special body of people—is rapidly becoming obsolete.

Is it not curious that the people who are chosen to represent us in ecumenical and inter-faith conversations always turn out to be very cautious and conservative characters who think like lawyers? In a world in which tradition is dying, we seem to feel safest when we are represented by extreme traditionalists. We like to be represented by people who are utterly unrepresentative of us. It is as if we very much want them to go on defending, on our behalf, positions that we no longer hold ourselves.

What then has happened? In the earliest times—or so we are told—religion was monocultural and henotheistic. Each people or *ethne* had their own language, their own sacred territory and their own god. Identities were clear-cut to such an extent that if you went to live in another territory, amongst other people, those new people became your people and their god your god. (See Ruth 1:15f.; *1* Samuel 26:19 etc.). The notion that religion is—or at least ideally should be—strictly ethnic and territorial has survived to this day. People still sometimes use terms like Christendom and Islam in a territorial way, and speak of lands like France and Italy as 'Roman Catholic countries'. Politicians in those countries do not find it at all easy to acknowledge publicly the fact that there may very soon be—and perhaps already are—more practising Muslims than practising Catholics in the home population. In Italy some years ago, politicians who were not themselves practising Catholics at all nevertheless found they simply could not bring themselves to attend the inauguration of Rome's first major mosque. They were accustomed to thinking of themselves as non-Catholics in a Catholic country, and somehow could not take in the thought that social change might be turning them into non-Muslims in a Muslim country.

Our thinking about true religion and territoriality has become oddly confused. For more than one-and-a-half millennia the Jews were in effect the principal and most obvious example of an ancient faith that had lost its own territory and now survived within Christendom, within Islam, and elsewhere in encapsulated form.[16] People identified themselves as Jews, and were identified, in every other way except through their possession of their own holy land. Your Jewishness was conveyed to you through your genealogy, your community-membership, your language, scriptures, customs and cultural tradition: but territory—no. The Jews were often regarded as a dispersed, homeless, fugitive people, living in a state of what seemed permanent diaspora, homelessness. The state of being exiled from one's proper sacred territory seemed pitiable. Then came the Restoration, the founding of the state of Israel, and a seemingly wonderful fulfilment of prophecy. But, fifty years later, not all Jews have wished to return, and visitors to Israel are astonished to find what a secular society it is and how little regard is paid to the Torah. Can Judaism not survive the fulfilment of its own hopes? Is the recovered possession of one's own holy land somehow now a religiously bad thing? In countries like the United States there has for some time been anxiety that the Jews in diaspora may disappear within half a century by marrying-out, and by complete assimilation into the host culture. But now we find that a worse danger threatens in the opposite direction: the Return to Israel fulfils Judaism—and then eclipses it, as all the precious old religious values of Judaism disappear into militant nationalist politics.

Judaism, then, seems to be caught between Scylla and Charybdis. In America and in 'the West' generally it threatens to become just one more strand in the new globalized world-historical culture, like Platonism. It will become simply part of the universal syllabus, part of everybody's heritage, and will no longer be or need to be embodied in a distinct visible human society. At the opposite extreme, Judaism also disappears in Israel. The ancient dream of a mono-ethnic theocratic state society cannot be realized in the modern world, except by turning religious values into political ones.

Islam is, of course, nowadays caught in just the same dilemma: and so too is Christianity. The ideal of 'a Christian country' is fading, disappearing. In Western society at large the Christian tradition has become just one more strand in everybody's cultural heritage. What survives of the Church is so drastically reduced that it no longer has any special claim to, nor expertise in, the old 'great' tradition. In which case, conversations between officially-nominated teams of Jewish and Christian representatives will be mainly exercises in denial. They will be conducted as if old-style distinct, homogeneous faith communities, in which traditional religious values are preserved intact, still exist—which is not the case, in a world where all of us alike are 'mediatized', immersed in the new media culture. And so long as we go on clinging to the memory of our lost closed worlds, for so long we will be failing to discuss the prospect that faces us all alike—both people who are ancestrally Jewish, and people who are ancestrally Christian—in the new globalized world-culture. At our interfaith conversations we try to reassure ourselves that we really are still different from each other and do still possess our own distinct 'identities'. But the reality is that the process of world-cultural assimilation is swallowing us both up. We are becoming more and more alike. All distinct ethnic and religious identities, of the old kind that we are so desperately nostalgic for, are rapidly vanishing.

This very painful example brings out the scale of today's religious crisis. We are right to have seen the Jews as 'a light to the nations', because certain universal structures of religious thought have been so clearly and even classically exemplified for us all by the Jews for so long. The central idea is that of a domain unified under a divine Monarch, a transcendent controlling principle and focus of loyalty that has instituted and now orders everything. The Monarch's power unifies everything and makes it all holy: the Holy Land, the Holy People, the sacred language, the Holy Books of the Law. There is a very clear line between the sacred and profane realms, and it is the line that separates insiders from outsiders; and all your various loyalties—to your people to your mother-tongue, to your land, to your holy city, to your God and so on—are fully synthesized.

Some such arrangement as this prevailed for most of the time around the world from the beginnings of agricultural civilization until about the year 1500 c.e. The Hebrew Bible describes with great clarity the (rather late) establishment of Israel's version of the system, and prints it almost indelibly upon our minds and hearts as the ideal to which we aspire. This is what we long for; this is how human beings should live. This is what it is to have an identity; this is what it is to know where you belong, who your friends are and who your enemies, and how you should live.

But it is all fast disappearing now, as I first realized when in 1980 I visited an Inuit (or 'Eskimo') primary school in Baffin Island and found that the syllabus, the culture, the language and even the pop music being imparted to the children was indistinguishable from that in the primary school which my own younger daughter was still attending in Cambridge. We cling to our identities—just because they are vanishing so rapidly. Much of religious talk and practice nowadays seems to consist of lamentations over, and rather ineffectual attempts to re-enact, all the things that we are now fast losing. Wouldn't it be better if we were to talk together about what is now coming upon all of us?

For is it not the case that our own tradition itself foresaw the globalization—the reversal of Babel—that we now see? The development of a single world-wide communications network, the emergence of a globally-dominant language, the English language, and the spread of a single ethic, based mainly upon the UN Charter and the Universal Declaration of Human Rights, all around the globe is surely a very significant religious event. The choice of its motto by the BBC, a lifetime ago, shows that this was once obvious; 'Nation shall speak peace unto nation'. But today, unfortunately, we are absorbed in trying to conserve our separate identities. You have never seen, and I at least have not seen, any recent piece of religious writing that welcomes globalization as Pentecost, as a fulfilment of ancient hopes. Why not? Are we missing something?

25

LEARNING TO LIVE WITHOUT
OBJECTIVE REALITY

Osama Bin Laden, the well-known terrorist leader and critic of Western culture, has sagely observed that whereas people in the West are oriented towards life, he and his followers are lovers of death. To him it is obvious that a life oriented towards death is morally superior, grander, more traditional and more in accord with the teachings of religion than a life that is content just to affirm life.

In a sense he is right, but as we will see, some of the implications of what he is saying are at first surprising. The doctrine that the good life is a life spent principally in thinking about and preparing for death is integral to Platonism and to Catholicism. In the Gospel, two of Jesus' disciples, James and John, ask for the chief places at his right hand and his left in his Kingdom. Jesus is pictured as telling them that they do not realize what they are asking for: 'Are you able to drink the cup that I drink, and to be baptized with the baptism that I am baptized with?'—meaning, my way is a way of suffering and death, the way of the confessor and the martyr. To achieve the goal that the religious person seeks one must be ready to embrace a very-unpleasant death. The Summum Bonum (supreme good) is located on the far side of that death.

There is more, because in our tradition not only philosophy and religion looked to death, but so in a sense did politics. In the days before the English 'Glorious Revolution' and the invention of liberal capitalism, great men who sought to increase their wealth and power viewed the sword as the only effective instrument for achieving that goal. Wealth was tied up with land, and land was ultimately gained and held by the sword. Kings were military leaders, and soldiering was regarded as a highly honourable profession. Young men were raised to a surprising degree in a military ethic, and even I still had to serve in the 'Cadet Corps' at my comfortable bourgeois school in the Home Counties of England. Men grew up with thoughts of dying for their country. I remember: I did.

In retrospect, our whole culture used to be oriented towards death to an astonishing degree, and it has taken centuries for us to become persuaded that the real wealth creator is not the great military leader like Napoleon, but the administrator like Colbert, the merchant, the free-trader, the engineer and the negotiator of international agreements. Turning our secular culture around so that it becomes oriented towards prosperity, peace and well-being in this life has been a struggle in the face of deep moral disapproval from death-oriented traditionalism. The military landowning class looked down upon 'trade', as the sword looks down upon the counter.

Even today we still have a long way to go. Even today, the call of religion is always a call *back*, back to the old ways, back to the ancestral home, language, virtues, customs, songs and grievances. When you wonder about your relation to religion and visit an old village church, you ponder the attractions of being immersed in the immemorial life of the folk, your forebears in the old agricultural civilization. You are getting into the mood of Thomas Gray's *Elegy Written in a Country Churchyard*: for you, it seems, the call of religion is a call back to an age less restless and highly-conscious than our own. You want to go back into the folk, into their anonymous slumbering conformity, into immanence and pure objectivity—in fact, into death, because what you really want is to become one of those who sleep in this churchyard.

Thus we naturally associate religion with a yearning to return into primal security and communal ease. We want to be immersed in dreaming comfort, in immanence and pure objectivity—in short, in death. But the religion of life commits us to exactly the opposite values. It says that the way our culture has developed, especially over the last four or five centuries, has committed us to critical thinking, to the loss of any readymade objective reality, to a high level of consciousness, and to the task of creating our own common human world and our own common values. The religion of life is an attempt to understand and to accept this relatively new vision of the human condition. We are more like artists than soldiers, now: we have to learn to live creatively and affirmatively. In the old kind of religion you saw life as a pilgrimage and you lived a disciplined itinerant life under rule, like a wandering philosopher, missionary or soldier. Happiness would come after the death you were seeking. In the new kind of religion you live a life that is materially probably much more settled, but you also live with and you must make something of a degree of scepticism and even nihilism that people in earlier times would have thought utterly unendurable. Life is hard work, a work of continuous renegotiation, compromise, revaluation. But it can now be more *intensely* lived and enjoyed than ever before. Why?—because after the death of all the old philosophical and religious ideologies that taught us to be suspicious of life and to distance ourselves from it, we now find that life is closer to us than breathing, nearer than hands and feet. Life is *us*, life is all this, now.

26

LIVING BY 'DYING', BY CONSTANTLY PASSING OUT INTO SYMBOLIC EXPRESSION

It is not easy to get into coherent form one's ideas about selfhood and action in time. The Bible sorts the whole question out with great force by attributing everything to God, and to him total mastery: 'For He spake the word, and they (the heavenly bodies) were made; He commanded and they were created'. God's utterance immediately creates facts that 'stand fast', and are 'established forever', and he himself remains the same, unaffected by his own activity. We humans cannot say as much as that. For us, in our own day, our conversation establishes a world of only transient fact, and we ourselves are also only the transient products of our own talk. Our sense-experience is fleeting, and our theories are subject to continual debate and revision, so that we have only a transient, compromise world. And that is all there is: transience rules.

We need a little more detail about how the solar living of the individual works, and here I still find useful a model that goes back as far as Schopenhauer, almost two hundred years ago. The individual human being is a compact bundle of emotional drives that constantly pour out, seeking expression. Just as they say that in your seventy-to-ninety-year lifespan your heart will beat just so many times, be it quickly or slowly, and you will draw breath so many times, be it quickly or slowly, so we seem to begin our lives with just so much intensely-compacted emotional energy that we are going to burn up during our whole lifespan. At first we burn very fiercely, and a baby's violent moods succeed each other vary rapidly. But gradually we slow down—so much, that I think I now take several months to burn up the amount of emotional energy that my one-year-old descendants expend in a single day.

These emotional, or as Freud calls them, 'instinctual' drives tend to come in paired opposites, and many of them readily fix upon external objects or patterns of behaviour through which they can be expended most easily. But in many, many cases objective gratification is not to be had: for example, the infant cannot hope actually to kill the object of its sudden storm of rage (although if the object *does* die, the young child may fancy that it has caused the death—the Freudian 'omnipotence of wishes'); but more often, one must be content with fantasy gratification of one's wishes, or with *symbolic gratification*. This happens especially where society, for the sake of civil peace and order, prohibits me from seizing for myself exactly who and what I desire, or where the environment I live in is too narrow and constricting to supply me with what I want. In such a case, where I cannot find my dream lover, I may have to be content with keeping a dog or writing *Jane Eyre*.

On this account, in a great deal of our cultural and religious activity we are seeking to relieve our feelings by discharging them through socially-acceptable symbolic outlets. If in art or religion I can find ways of expressing myself that are powerful enough to relieve several different conflicting feelings at once, then I can say that by making this artwork or by going through that ritual I can 'get myself together': I get a feeling of relief and of wholeness or integration. And of course I attribute the very highest value to the objects on which I can expend my strongest feelings of love, and awe, and admiration, and gratitude.

This broadly-Freudian account suggests that all through our lives we need to engage in creative, expressive activity through which we can perhaps enrich the common human world and at the same time find personal salvation, and it provides the background against which we can elaborate the theory of solar living.

Solar living, then, precisely reverses the traditional Western account of the religious life. It is living by continual self-outing, or expression—which explains why modern people attach so much importance to **coming out with it**, *declaring* themselves, and generally feeling able uninhibitedly to be themselves in public without concealment. But since the Middle Ages in the West the individual's religious life has commonly moved in the opposite direction, being described as a second 'interior' or 'spiritual' life, a life of hidden inwardness in which the soul related itself to the invisible God who was its Ground and its End. The language used implied rather sharp distinctions between body and soul, and between outer appearance and inner reality. Everyone was an amphibian, living simultaneously in two worlds or at two levels, like an actor or a spy. Your apparent, outward or bodily life was a life of social relations with other people in this visible world, but at the same time you were also withholding part of yourself in order to live a second, inward life in which you continually referred everything to the Eternal God. To do religion you sought solitude and stillness, sat still, shut your eyes, recollected yourself, and turned into your own interior mental space.

I reject this traditional Western picture utterly, insisting that there is no interior core-self with a hotline to Eternity. We just are our own outer lives in time, and our public life of self-expression just *is* our religious life. There is only the outward, passing show of things. Our language is a single, outsideless, human continuum, and the world that our language gives us is also a single outsideless continuum. There is only one world, and only one self. We are not dual, amphibian creatures, and religion is not concerned with any other world than the everyday world. Religion is simply our own activity in trying to get ourselves into the most affirmative and productive relation to life that is attainable. That is not easy, however: we will not get it right unless we have learnt to look head-on at the insubstantiality, chanciness and transience of everything—including ourselves—and have found the courage and the faith to say Yes to life in the face of all *that*. All of which, I warn you, is going to be very tough.

'The objective world around me now looks solid enough', you may say, 'and my own established character seems to be set very firm. So why are you trying to reduce everything to a passing show of events?' I reply that it's a matter of analysis. The objective world you see around you now is inherited; it is the residue of the human past, the deposit of people's perception, differentiation, theorizing and occasional redevelopment of their environment. The English language as you and I use it today is similarly a very large collection of human customs accumulated by our predecessors over the centuries, and your present self is likewise the accumulated residue of your own past bits of behaviour. In every case, accumulated custom and practice generates a feeling of objective reality, and that's all.

'But what about long-term planning, and the achievement of great works?' you may persist: 'Your solar living is so concentrated upon life in the present moment that it makes me wonder how anyone can ever get anything lasting done.' I reply that solar living is indeed an attempt to live as intensely and creatively as one can, *now*. We live in times when the collective human future on the large scale has become very uncertain, and I personally have reached an age at which I can no longer count upon, or plan with confidence for, any very long-term future. So like a painter I just sink myself into the work that is immediately to hand, get on with that, and leave the future to look after itself. It is nothing to us: we have lost the glorious futures people used to believe in. Meanwhile, solar living is eschatological living, living as if one lives in the last days. You mind your own business, do your own thing for its own sake, and do without the big picture. We have lost the big picture, the old grand narrative of universal redemption. For me, at least, *now* is all I seem to have left. So I am trying to **make the most of it** (one of the best of all the **it**-idioms, by the way).

27

OUR WORLD, OUR COMMUNAL
WORK OF FOLK ART

Our chief business, all our lives, is with managing our relations with each other, with other features of the world, with It All, and with Life—and especially with the basic limits of life, its temporality, its contingency (which means that it is liable to throw almost anything at us, quite unexpectedly), and its finitude. In developing their **life-skills** people nowadays call upon the help of **life coaches** rather than priests, but the whole business of learning to cope with **It All** is in fact religious. In this connexion we develop a wide range of common practices and symbols, and one may usefully define a people's culture as the whole ensemble of their communally-possessed and generally-intelligible signs. Within their culture as a whole, a people's *religion* is then the public stock of currently-used symbols and practices through which they express their common understanding of life, cope with life, and celebrate it.

In modern society we have a huge quantity of religious language and symbolism, left over from the past and now scattered across the whole face of language. Because religious symbols are after all the most memorable and powerful of all symbols, they are very hard to forget. They linger on, admittedly retaining a certain poetic usefulness and charm, to the point where eventually they become a nuisance. They block our vision, they prevent us from seeing things clearly, and they allow us to postpone the most important religious task of all, namely that we shall find the courage nakedly and autologously[17] to confront, on our own and for ourselves, the truth of the human condition. The long dominance of tradition-directed thinking has made us into pathological religious *hoarders*. Our culture is cluttered up with picturesque old junk from the past—stuff to do with the supernatural world above, with sin, sacrifice, and salvation, with belief in life after death, and so on—and while our heads are full of such clutter we will not be able to get clear about anything. A religious purge is urgently needed.

For many years now I have been attempting to persuade my readers, and myself, to throw out the junk—that is, consciously to abandon and get rid of all the inherited religious language and symbolism that blocks our heads because it no longer does any real religious work. To follow this path is to follow what traditional spirituality described as the Purgative Way. Very much as scientific knowledge is advanced by the systematic criticism and purging of what currently passes for knowledge, so in religion too we need to criticize and expel all the illusory and dysfunctional religious material we have inherited. As we become more and more naked and beliefless, we begin to experience the dissolution of the self. The aim is eventually to look coolly and without any self-deception at the truth of the human condition. We learn to see more clearly what life is, and on what basis one can nowadays live a life of one's own. Like a child that has just learnt how to ride a bicycle without any support, we have to learn the trick of trusting life, so that we can plunge recklessly into the empty flux of existence, and let ourselves go with it. We have to learn to trust life, love life, and enjoy life, while life lasts.

It all sounds simple, but it is utterly terrifying. One has to go through the Nihil, through something that really does feel like death and rebirth. But on the far side lies the possibility of religious renewal, and indeed a wider cultural renewal. For going all the way into nihilism (perhaps with the help of the modern philosophers—Kant, Nietzsche, Heidegger) teaches us the extent to which the world about us is a very mixed, complicated, sometimes beautiful and sometimes shabby and muddled work of folk art, evolved piecemeal by us over several tens of thousands of years.

This elementary truth, that the world has only ever been seen from the human point of view, or rather, that the only world we ever have known or *can* know is a world that has already been construed and in effect *constructed* by us, has very often been concealed by religion and philosophy. Shamans, mediums, ecstatic prophets, visionaries, and hearers of revelations have supposed that in an altered state of consciousness they were getting a higher and superhuman truth of things piped directly from the heavenly world above into their own heads. Metaphysicians have supposed that human reason, suitably trained, can somehow be employed to transcend Nature and lift us above ourselves. But when we understand the radical dependence of all propositional thought—true-or-false thought—upon language we are immediately liberated from such illusions. The world is always *our* world: the only world we can ever have access to is a world that we have already made our own. Have you not understood that the very word **world** means 'the age or the times of a man' (*weoruld*), as in a familiar expression like 'Shakespeare's world'? It means his times, his 'age', or his setting-in-life. So our world is a huge many-layered historical deposit like a great cliff, the accumulated product of tens of thousands of years of human talk; and your individual world, being in many ways a selection of bits of our common world with which you have gradually come to surround yourself, is at least in part a reflection of what you are. Thus we can replace the popular ideas of *your self* and *the world* with the more accurate and less-misleading ideas of **your life** and **your world**. Your life and your world are the subjective and the objective surfaces of one 'interface', the plane of your living.

We now glimpse the possibility of a new 'framing' for religious thought. Kant introduced the idea of a thorough critical appraisal of knowledge, and Marx introduced the idea of an equally thorough critique of human power-relationships in society. What, then, of the possibility of a critique of Life? Subjectively, this would amount to my critique of my own life—in effect, a continuation of traditional ideas of self-examination. I should try to appraise the way I live, the values by which I live, and the overall tendency or orientation of my life. But there is also the larger, objective question of world-critique, when I begin to think critically not just about my own immediately-surrounding life-world, but also about the larger, common life-world that we humans have constructed around ourselves.

This last suggestion has been in the air for some time. For about 50 years, people in the older generation have been saying 'What kind of world have we made: what sort of world are we now handing over to you in the next generation?' The two World Wars, and the subsequent controversies about reconstruction after them, made many ordinary people aware for the first time of their own responsibility for history and for world-making. So I am pretty sure that the sense that 'we' as a generation are responsible for our own collective world-making begins only in the year 1960 or thereabouts.

Today the whole issue has suddenly been made much more urgent, and has been stepped up a gear, by our dawning realization that global warming and climate change are not just trendy topics of conversation, but are 'for real'. We are beginning to think about the way our science and technology, and our industrial and financial systems, have led us to build our common world. In the present growing crisis we are sure to be reminded of the critique of modern technology and related topics in Heidegger's philosophy, and we may go on to think about the possibility of a religious **world-critique** that revives in a modern form the old idea that the whole of our world and our way of life is subject to Divine Judgement.

The starting point for such a comprehensive Critique of our whole world of life is obvious enough. We begin by pointing out the strange 'angelism' of early-modern Reason in the philosophy of Descartes. The scientific observer, disengaged, disembodied, peeks into the material world as if from a point somewhere, anywhere, outside it. The scientific reasoner-mathematician tracks the divine Reason as he works out the laws of nature. And this oddly spirit-like conception of the scientist prepares the way for the later technological conception of the world as so much inert, available raw material out there, which we can exploit as we wish. If we are spirits, what we love most is freedom, and power, and what the Germans used to call 'world-mastery'. So we developed our technology and our industrial society in that interest, with consequences that are now coming home to us. And this should be sufficient to show that the new religion of life may well be capable of developing a large-scale religious critique of the human world as it now stands.

There is one *caveat*. The negative critique, asking how and where we went wrong, is easy and has largely been done already by Heidegger, by Jacques Ellul, and by various others.[18] Much more important, *and much more difficult*, is the task of persuading the mass of the people that we really can do much better—that before we destroy ourselves we can and must change over en masse to a whole range of new ideas about the self, about Life, about the world, and about love, world-love and eternal happiness.

Presentism

28

NO TIME LIKE THE PRESENT

In philosophy, the term 'presentism' is currently used to describe a philosophical position that every young person considers at one time or another, namely the doctrine that only the present is real. The past has gone, becoming instantly irrecoverable the moment it slips away; and the future is not yet. So there is only the present (and an awkward question: if the past does not exist, how can statements about it be true or false?). But then what *is* the present? Is it an interface with no depth, a moving line, a knife-edge between what hasn't yet come and what has already gone? It seems that the present moment must have a certain bandwidth or thickness so as to allow our restless eyes time to flicker over the scene before us, and our brains time to construct their pictures of the world as it is just *now*. So how much thickness, then? I have usually guessed: approximately 0.1 seconds. But then we may be troubled by second thoughts to the effect that the sheer amount of apparatus that we use in building our current picture of the world, interpreting it, and deciding what we are to do, is very large. It includes all of our language, our knowledge, and our experience of the way things usually go; and much of this apparatus has taken millennia to evolve within past human societies. This suggests that we always begin, at least, by seeing the present in the light of our whole accumulated past—which is therefore surely in some sense still around and still influential. The present may then be viewed as a top layer now being added on to the inherited world-as-we-have-built-it-up-so-far. And if we are thus led to think of the accumulated past as being still around, we can more easily see how statements about it may be true or false. By this route then we have come to a way of looking at time which starts from the distinction between the perfect and the imperfect tenses. The world as it has been 'perfected' so far is a great layer cake made of all our past interpretations of it, laid down one above another. The present then is the leading edge, or the top surface of the cake, where today's interpretations are being laid down over all the previous ones. As for the imperfect, the term refers to what is not yet. It may be scheduled, or predicted, or prophesied or whatever, but as yet it has not actually taken place. It is yet to come.

This is just one of the many models that we may experiment with in trying to think about time. A recent computer word-count found that *time* is the most commonly used general noun in the English language,[19] and everyone must have noticed at one time or another what an elusive and difficult topic it is. But on any view, the present is where the action is. Inevitably, there is always an argument between people who want to stress the extent to which what is presently going on has to be seen in the light of the past and is duly laid down on top of the past, the world as it has been accumulated so far, and, on the other hand, all those people who don't want to be tied down by history. They want to break with the past, and to refresh our perceptions. The first group sound like traditionalists who want to stay within what we have been taught to regard as the real, and the second group sound like Wordsworthians who want to escape from **the real world**, the world that is too much with us, and to recover the joyous innocent freshness of childhood experience. The first group are like Victorian historicists who see themselves as having a long historically-evolved tradition behind them, and the second group are like Modernist painters of the *Fauve* and *Blaue Reiter* groups who love bright colours, the innocent eye, and a new beginning.

In religion there has been a similar reaction against those whose hope of eventually gaining eternal happiness depends upon their belief in a vast Grand Narrative myth of cosmic Fall and Redemption. The story (as they see it) coheres with their society's general world-picture, much of it is taught in Holy Scripture, and, so far as it bears upon the individual person nowadays, it again broadly fits with her experience. The individual feels entitled to say: 'That's the story of *my* life, too! I have a place in that great plan, and am assured that if I am a faithful, conforming member of the holy people, I will personally have a part in the final Glory at the end of history.'

For this type of classical Western or Latin Christianity, the individual's sense of religious meaning in her life depended upon her conviction that the Grand Narrative of cosmic history was true, and that her own life really did fit into it. Her salvation was thus certified to her by the Cosmic Narrator himself, via the Church. Fine—until about the time of Milton and Bunyan, the reign of King Charles II, the establishment of the Royal Society and the work of Isaac Newton. Since then, the old Grand Narrative has undergone the death by a thousand qualifications, and nothing is now left of it.

In response to this very-large-scale intellectual crisis, religious thought flew to the opposite pole, and began to claim that the verification of our religious beliefs need not wait until the end of history. It could happen now, in the individual's present experience. This claim was made especially clearly, and in a way evidently modelled upon 'experimental verification' in natural philosophy, by the early English Evangelicals of the mid-18th century. They stressed personal conversion, personal experience of saving Grace, and visible conversion of life as together supplying clear, present-tense, and even *public* evidence of the truth of their faith.

Of course, Evangelicals were and are scriptural 'Fundamentalists', who closely tied together their daily study of the Bible with their daily devotions, so that nobody could doubt exactly what religious tenets his religious experience verified; but what is important for the present argument is the Evangelical conviction that the truth of one's personal salvation could be verified *here and now* within the subjectivity—the personal experience—of the individual. On this point, at least, the Evangelicals were not mere reactionaries, but were attempting a positive response to the intellectual challenge of modernity.

Thus in Newton's day the vindication of faith had long been seen in cosmic Grand Narrative terms; but then only two or three generations later everything had become contracted down and refocused upon the single individual's experience of divine Grace, personal conversion, joy, and the Assurance of salvation, all in the present moment. Both ends of the spectrum are arguably founded in the writing of Calvin himself.

In several other religions, including most notably Buddhism, the same contrast is made. Some writers describe vast cosmic cycles of rebirth and decay, and speak of the individual as needing thousands of lifetimes to attain final release; but then another tradition says that by the right kind of act of faith and self-surrender it is possible to achieve *satori* instantly.

Today we are acutely aware of the quite-recent final collapse of all the Grand Narratives, both religious and political, that described a world-historical movement towards final salvation or general human liberation at the end of time. Nietzsche was one of the first to say eloquently and very forcefully that all stories that picture world-history as being steered towards the fulfilment of a great Purpose are dead, and he naturally drew the conclusion that from now on we have to find 'the meaning of life' here and now, in the present moment. But Nietzsche's ideas took a century to win general acceptance, which came only with the sudden intellectual and moral collapse of Communism at the end of the 1980s. The last great Grand Narrative had suddenly died. Liberal and Christian versions of the same story were evidently not in very good health either. Since then, there has been something of a turn towards the present moment, subjective experience and 'spirituality' in religious thought.

I offer all this as an explanation of why I see the new Religion of Ordinary Life as directing attention in the first place to the individual—to the individual's questions about life, the individual's sense of being threatened by pessimism and very clouded prospects for the future, the individual's *present* need to find a way of coming to terms with life's permanent limits, and so to the message that the individual can here and now live life to the full, and find eternal joy in life in the present moment. To many critics it seems that I am repeating the excessive individualism of the older 'world faiths' which two thousand years ago put the great question in the form 'What must I do to be saved?' My reply points out the context in which we now live: intellectual nihilism, individual death as simple extinction, and a bleak outlook for humankind as a whole. In the face of all that, I need first of all to find a basis on which I can live, and live well *now*. I need a *modus vivendi* for myself before I can even begin to think about placing myself in a wider society.

Notes

1. These books include the Everyday Speech trilogy, published by the SCM Press of London: *The New Religion of Life in Everyday Speech*, 1999, *The Meaning of It All in Everyday Speech*, 1999, and *Kingdom Come in Everyday Speech*, 2000. A follow-up trilogy then appeared from the Polebridge Press of Santa Rosa, California: *Life, Life*, 2003, *The Way to Happiness*, 2005, and *The Great Questions of Life*, 2006. Other ideas were first broached in *Solar Ethics*, SCM Press 1995, reprinted 2005, *Philosophy's Own Religion*, SCM Press 2000, *Emptiness and Brightness*, Polebridge Press 2001, and *The Old Creed and the New*, SCM Press 2006.

2. We should disregard the journalistic nonsense that, on the basis of a revival of desperately-low-quality 'fundamentalist' religion, assures us that the Secularization Thesis has been falsified, and 'God is back'. In fact, philosophers have not found fresh and compelling arguments for the existence of God and the supernatural world, and biblical critics have not suddenly discovered that scripture really is inerrant, and does after all teach in full the orthodox dogmas of the Trinity and the Incarnation. On the contrary, the intellectual standing of all versions of orthodox, traditional religion has continued to deteriorate steadily, and no modern religious leader dares to write a full systematic defence of the orthodoxy he is required to guard. The excellent historian of philosophy R.H. Popkin thought that the last full-scale defence of the Christian philosophy of God and the world was that of Cudworth in 1678. Any writer of newspaper pieces who thinks that the situation has recently changed for the better should be disregarded.

I write as a Christian (or post-christian) theologian, but other religions are no better off.

3. There are many interesting nineteenth-century examples of writers who lose their faith, stop talking about 'God', and instead start using the word 'life' as a replacement. John Ruskin is one of the best. Others range from Hardy to Lawrence.

4. On this, see Hugh Rayment-Pickard, *Impossible God*, and my *Impossible Loves*.

5. Michael Payne and John Schad, *Life.After.Theory*.

6. For this idea see both Dante and Milton. Angels are transparent: you can 'read' their thoughts. But no language is involved, because what happens is that the pure concepts in their heads are instantly tracked by matching pure concepts in yours!

7. Cupitt, *The Religion of Being* and *The Revelation of Being*, both SCM Press 1998.

8. *The Letters of Vincent van Gogh*. For a sample, see two letters to Émile Bernard: 23 June 1888 and c. 20 November 1889; pp.368–372 and 467–473.

9. The contents of this section are inevitably closely related to my book *Impossible Loves*.

10. The ideas that follow in this section were first broached in *Solar Ethics*, 1995, but have been developed a little since then.

11. The ideas in this section were originally launched in *The New Christian Ethics*, 1988, but—again—have developed a little over the years.

12. The recent success of Sam Harris, *The End of Faith*, indicates that many secular liberals are coming to feel that they have been too tolerant of religion for too long.

13. Amongst historians of religion and 'comparative religionists' the one whose outlook is closest to my own and to the themes of this book is the late Trevor Ling: see his *A History of Religion East and West*.

14. In this connection I will mention the painting of Camille Pissarro; but of course a claim could no doubt be made on behalf of many another, much earlier.

15. For 'hauntology', 'spectral theology' etc., see Jacques Derrida, *Specters of Marx*. For the background theme of this section, that the Incarnation was *itself* God's choice of death and the reduction of the whole of Christianity to secular humanism, see the many writings of T. J. J. Altizer.

16. The Parsees of India are another example.

17. For this neologism see my *The Old Creed and The New*.

18. See Martin Heidegger, *The Question Concerning Technology*. This famous essay raises an important question for our current debates about global warming and climate change: If it was the technological mindset that got us into this mess, why are we assuming that more technology can get us out of it?

There is also a further question to be put to Heidegger himself: Tool-using amongst animals is older than mankind, and has clearly influenced the evolution of the human hand with its opposed thumb. Perhaps some use of technology was from the very first necessary for human survival: perhaps technology made man, rather than the other way round? What can Heidegger say to *that*?

19. 'Life' came ninth.

Books Referred to

In this book I have attempted a systematic statement of the leading ideas in the main line of my thinking, as they stand today in what is presumably their final form. Various sidelines are left unmentioned, and I list below those books of mine which first broached ideas that are used in this book. Otherwise, I list only books that are expressly referred to, and also some other items to which I am indebted whether more or less explicitly.

Robert L. Arrington and Mark Addis (edd.), *Wittgenstein and Philosophy of Religion*, London and New York: Routledge, 2001.

Thomas J.J. Altizer, *The Self-Embodiment of God*, New York: Harper and Row, 1977.

———, *History and Apocalypse*, Albany, NY: State University of New York, 1985.

———, *Genesis and Apocalypse*, Louisville, KY: Westminster/John Knox, 1990.

———, *The Contemporary Jesus*, Albany, NY: SUNY Press, 1997.

Andrew Bowie, *From Romanticism to Critical Theory: The Philosophy of German Literary Theory*, London and New York: Routledge, 1997.

Don Cupitt, *The New Christian Ethics*, London: SCM Press 1988, Xpress reprint, 1993.

———, *Creation Out of Nothing*, London: SCM Press and Philadelphia: Trinity Press International, 1990.

———, *The Time Being*, London: SCM Press, 1992.

———, *After All*, London: SCM Press, 1994, reprinted 1995.

———, *Solar Ethics*, London: SCM Press, 1995, reprinted 2005.

———, *The New Religion of Life in Everyday Speech*, London: SCM Press, 1999.

———, *The Meaning of It All in Everyday Speech*, London: SCM Press, 1999.

———, *Kingdom Come in Everyday Speech*, London: SCM Press, 2000.

———, *Philosophy's Own Religion*, London: SCM Press, 2000.

———, *Emptiness and Brightness*, Santa Rosa, CA: Polebridge Press, 2001.

———, *Life, Life*, Santa Rosa, CA: Polebridge Press, 2003.

———, *The Way to Happiness*, Santa Rosa, CA: Polebridge Press, 2005.

———, *The Great Questions of Life*, Santa Rosa, CA: Polebridge Press, 2006.

———, *The Old Creed and the New*, London: SCM Press, 2006.

———, *Impossible Loves*, Santa Rosa, CA: Polebridge Press, 2007

Jacques Derrida, *Specters of Marx: The State of the Debt, The Work of Mourning and the New International*, trans. Peggy Kamuf, New York: Routledge, 1994.

Emile L. Fackenheim, *The Religious Dimension in Hegel's Thought*, Chicago: University of Chicago Press, 1967, reprinted 1982.

Giles Fraser, *Redeeming Nietzsche: On the Piety of Unbelief*, London and New York: Routledge, 2002.

Lloyd Geering, *The World to Come: From Christian Past to Global Future*, Santa Rosa, CA: Polebridge Press, 1999.

———, *Tomorrow's God: How We Create Our Worlds*, Wellington, NZ: Bridget Williams, 1994; reprinted Santa Rosa, CA: Polebridge Press, 2000.

Richard Harland, *Superstructuralism*, London: Methuen, 1987.

Sam Harris, *The End of Faith: Religion, Terror and the Future of Reason*, New York: W. W. Norton, 2004.

Martin Heidegger, *The Question Concerning Technology and Other Essays*, trans. William Lovitt, New York: Harper and Row, 1977.

F. R. Leavis, *The Living Principle: English as a Discipline of Thought*, London: Chatto and Windus, 1975.

Ronald de Leeuw (ed.), *The Letters of Vincent van Gogh*, London and New York: Penguin Books, 1997.

Trevor Ling, *A History of Religion East and West*, London and New York: Macmillan, 1968, reprinted 1974.

Richard Mason, *The God of Spinoza*, Cambridge: Cambridge University Press, 1997, reprinted 1999, 2001.

John Milbank, *Theology and Social Theory: Beyond Secular Reason*, Oxford: Blackwell, 1990.

———, with Catherine Pickstock and Graham Ward (edd.), *Radical Orthodoxy: A New Theology*, London: Routledge, 1999 (see footnote 49 on p. 37).

Steven Mithen, *The Singing Neanderthals: The Origins of Music, Language, Mind and Body*, London: Weidenfeld and Nicholson, 2005.

George Pattison, *The Later Heidegger*, London: Routledge, 2000.

Michael Payne and John Shad (edd.), *Life.After.Theory*, London: Continuum, 2003.

Hugh Rayment-Pickard, *Impossible God: Derrida's Theology*, Aldershot: Ashgate, 2003.

Arthur Schopenhauer, *Parerga and Paralipomena*, trans. E. F. J. Payne, Oxford: the Clarendon Press, 1974, Volume Two, Essay XV, 'On Religion'.

Ludwig Wittgenstein, *Philosophical Investigations*, trans. G. E. M. Anscombe, Oxford: Blackwell, 1953.

Index

LaVergne, TN USA
17 March 2011
220598LV00005B/76/P